HENRY JAMES
AND MASCULINITY

HENRY JAMES
AND MASCULINITY

The Man at the Margins

Kelly Cannon

St. Martin's Press
New York

First published in the United States of America in 1994

Printed in the United States of America
Design: Acme Art, Inc., New York

ISBN 0-312-10405-7

Library of Congress Cataloging-in-Publication Data

Cannon, Kelly.
    Henry James and masculinity : the man at the margins / Kelly
Cannon.
        p. cm.
    Includes bibliographical references (p.) and index.
    ISBN 0-312-10405-7
    1. James, Henry, 1843-1916—Knowledge—Psychology. 2. James,
Henry, 1843-1916—Characters—Men. 3. Masculinity (Psychology) in
literature. 4. Men in literature. I. Title.
PS2127.P8C36 1993
813'.4—dc20   93-30200
                        FTW   CIP

                    AFD9011

CONTENTS

To my family
for their continuing
love and encouragement

PREFACE

While Henry James may strike one as intentionally difficult, he intends to be so not out of malice—not to test our patience nor to remind us of our ignorance—but to remind his readers of the complexity of life. That the ever mysterious component of life known as sexuality should appear in his fiction only obliquely when it appears at all does not attest to its lack of significance, but rather to the difficult placement of sexuality in life and art. James's art attests to the discomfort of sexual codes that run against the grain, and to the undeniable fact of their existence. How is one to acknowledge such "marginal" behavior in others? How is one to respond to these urges in oneself? While it may be shocking to think that James would entertain these questions, recent biographies explain his avidity for the subject.

My interest in Henry James came first from his exquisite style, that endless subtlety that James Baldwin praised in his predecessor. To then find within this prose a purpose that required subtlety for its discursive survival was gratifying to me on an aesthetic and personal level. James's fiction invites pleasurable rereading even after years of study. I hope that my work will illuminate the significance of his work for our time and for generations to come.

Many thanks to Linda Wagner-Martin, who assisted me not only with her editorial skills but also with her personal expression of professionalism. She is responsible for a perspective, what James would be pleased to call a "way of seeing." I wish also to acknowledge Everett Emerson for his familiarity with biographical facts and literary criticism that one must checkpoint if one is to discuss this writer and his work. My discussions with Kimball King enriched my understanding of James's defense of the imagination as a civilizing element. I also thank Townsend Ludington and Fred Hobson for their sound advice on textual matters.

As for the friendships that sustained me during the several years that I worked on this project, I gratefully acknowledge Ben Devane for his affection, Steve Kennedy for heartfelt talks on life and literature, and Dianne Chambers and Paul Crumbley for the voice of colleagues who understand.

They had from an early hour made up their mind that society was, luckily, unintelligent, and the margin allowed them by this had fairly become one of their commonplaces.

—*"The Beast in the Jungle"*

HENRY JAMES
AND MASCULINITY

—

Introduction

The life and work of Henry James offer a wealth of impressions to readers with eyes for the unconventional: the author and many of his male characters defy stereotypes of masculinity, asking in their varied voices if culture allows for deviation. Such exceptional behavior, however, does not always meet with reader approval. Take for example Lambert Strether, the protagonist of *The Ambassadors*. While James intends Strether to be a sympathetic character, several critics have found him lacking in male aggression and therefore unappealing. He has been variously described as timid, passive, delicate, sissified, and immoral.[1] A Strether-type male makes many readers uncomfortable because he avoids heterosexual entanglements to the satisfaction of his own eccentricities. James unsettles rather than appeases the reader's longing for conventional manhood.

Characters in James's fiction who defy masculine stereotypes are numerous: Rowland Mallet in *Roderick Hudson* (1875), Ralph Touchett of *The Portrait of a Lady* (1881), Hyacinth Robinson of *The Princess Casamassima* (1886), the narrator in *The Aspern Papers* (1888), the tutor and the pupil in the short story "The Pupil" (1891), the narrator in "The Figure in the Carpet" (1896), young Miles in *The Turn of the Screw* (1898), the narrator in "The Tree of Knowledge" (1900), Lambert Strether of *The Ambassadors* (1903), and John Marcher in "The Beast in the Jungle" (1903). The frequent occurrence of this marginal type suggests James's consciousness of alternative masculinity and an awareness that he was creating a world substantively different from the typically masculine world one reads about in conventional fiction or experiences in the workaday world.

An examination of the theme of masculinity in James's work entails a division of "early" and "late" along the lines of an increasing sophistication of style that achieves full force in the mid-1890s when James adopted what he called his "dramatic style." An increasing ambiguity of idea and expression accompanies these later works, which, according to Ruth Bernard Yeazell, turn on "mystery and delayed revelation" in a style that wishes to "uncover the 'literal' " at the same time that it "wishes to rename and transform it" (Yeazell, "Henry James," 685). The later style paradoxically reveals as it conceals, teasing the reader with partial images that suggest rather than name, by way of ellipsis, abstraction, and metaphor. "Through the medium of 'metaphoric indirection,' " Yeazell continues, one can identify James's late style by "the impulse toward evasion and postponement, articulating the space of imaginative free play" (Yeazell, "Henry James," 685). More and more toward the end of James's career, his texts defy absolute interpretation, asking the reader not to find, but to imagine.

From this vantage point, James appears thoroughly modern: one step ahead of the times, unconventional, in-between.[2] Far from offering absolutes about reality, James's ambiguity points to the modern age, with its shifting notions of "truth." In this light, James becomes less associated with moralism, Americanism, and synthesis; and more closely aligned with Europeanism, fragmentation, and contradiction (Freedman, *Professions*, xvi, 250). James's life and work chronicle the loss of absolutes, lost because they are fictional, inadequate because they are exclusive, in need of revision. He explores with growing interest the inadequacy of language to express a person's thoughts and feelings, the failure of ideologies to offer believers lasting happiness, and society's neglect of individual freedom.

Considering the modernity of his later work, it should come as no surprise that much post-structuralist attention to James focuses on the late fiction to the exclusion of earlier works. However, inclusion of both early and late works is necessary to illustrate the continuum of development in James's treatment of marginal behavior.[3] In earlier works, James tends to neglect his marginal males by displacing them to the margins of the text, thus avoiding any thorough examination of their masculinity. Only in later texts does he center his marginal characters sufficiently to allow complex examination.

The layered prose of later works allowed James to weave questionable themes into the text, themes that he dared not reveal in the sparer style of his earlier works. This increasing attention to marginality in the fiction speaks volumes about its creator. Conscious or unconscious, the later focus on marginality implies a creative impulse in James to unite art with his personal life. In what might appear as nothing more than stylistic development, James packed his later fiction more and more with what "matters," often at personal risk. (For the purposes of this study, earlier works will include, for instance, *Roderick Hudson* and *The Princess Casamassima;* transitional works, *The Aspern Papers* and "The Figure in the Carpet"; and later works, *The Turn of the Screw, The Ambassadors,* and "The Beast in the Jungle.")

The ever-increasing complexity of style in the later works invites alternative, even subversive, readings. One of James's rare pronouncements on the subversive element in literature appears in his essay "The Future of the Novel" (1901), where he notes the imperative of art to move forward in order to remain relevant to the consumer. He writes, "It is certain that there is no real health for any art . . . that does not move a step in advance of its farthest follower" (Veeder, *Art of Criticism,* 250). By acknowledging the need to advance just ahead of the "farthest follower," James is certainly no rebel; his revolution would be another's impediment, slow and tedious. Nonetheless, he unsettles society in his attempt to "move a step in advance," undermining convention by subtle, even devious means, in order to reorient values.

For instance, James's position on sexual mores is at best obscure. At first glance, he is one of the least "sexual" of writers, having fabricated a "gilded surface" that keeps the conventional reader from "excessive confrontation with the vulgar" (Yeazell, "Henry James," 688). Indeed, writers whom James admired, like Dickens and Scott, pleased him precisely because they avoided describing sexual activity. He writes in "The Future of the Novel," "I cannot so much as imagine Dickens and Scott *without* the 'love-making' left, as the phrase is, out. They were, to my perception, absolutely right . . . practically not to deal with it" (249). Novels from the past rightly avoided what was not an issue, accurately reflecting a time when frank discussion of sexuality, even in academic terms, was socially unacceptable.

Yet in "The Future of the Novel," James goes on to say that times have changed: "The novel is older, and so are the young" (249). Society was maturing in sexual matters, breaking the silence about an issue that had once been confined to the bedroom. For fiction to achieve maturity as an art form, it would have to discuss sexuality, which until that time had been "an immense omission in our fiction." But how was the author to deal with sexuality in a way satisfying to the interests of a more "mature" society while not abandoning decorum altogether? James's works appease both demands through a "double impulse to uncover and conceal," a "tension between an avid curiosity about the 'vulgar' facts and a wish to keep them at a distance," to refine them into what *The Sacred Fount* calls "a perfect palace of thought" (Yeazell, "Henry James," 684). In the pages where sex appears most absent, James assures its hidden presence. One example is the well-concealed sexual tension between Ralph Touchett and Isabel Archer. Another is the relationship between Maria Gostrey and Lambert Strether, whose language becomes hopelessly bound up in double entendre; their language means most what they would deny most emphatically—sexual desire. There is also homosexual tension: Lambert Strether's ardor for the fine physical specimen of Chad Newsome, the love between student and teacher in "The Pupil," and Hyacinth Robinson's fascination with Paul Muniment. As double entendre, the text signifies sexuality only for the willing reader.

In this Bakhtinian dialogue that feeds the reader's imagination only as he or she is prepared to receive it, James's fiction weaves a tapestry that wanders erotically and sometimes dangerously from acceptable territory into the margins, a place of existence without record, peopled by those individuals excluded from the pages of both history and art. A later American writer, James Baldwin, would find a kindred spirit in Henry James, recognizing a mutual goal to seek out "the reality of others" (Weatherby, *James Baldwin*, 85). Baldwin appropriately prefaced his novel *Another Country* with a statement made by James concerning the "others":

> They strike one, above all, as giving no account of themselves in terms already consecrated by human use; to this inarticulate state they probably form, collectively, the most unprecedented of monuments; abysmal the mystery of what they think, what they feel, what they want, what they suppose themselves to be saying.

These are characters whose inner lives stood unarticulated by themselves or others that James chose to chronicle loyally and insistently, however indirect his record may be.

As a corollary to his interest in the margins of society, James had long admired the European writers Charles Sainte-Beuve and Ivan Turgenev, who exemplified for him the condition of being "in-between" (Veeder, *Art of Criticism*, 2), inhabiting the ambiguous space between culturally defined femininity and masculinity. As James wrote of Sainte-Beuve,

> There is something feminine in his tact, his penetration, his subtlety and pliability, his rapidity of transition, his magical divinations, his sympathies and antipathies, his marvelous art of insinuation, of expressing himself by fine touches and of adding touch to touch. But all this side of the feminine genius was re-enforced by faculties of quite another order—faculties of the masculine stamp; the completeness, the solid sense, the constant reason, the moderation, the copious knowledge, the passion for exactitude and for general considerations. ("Sainte-Beuve," 27)

James adheres to social constructs in defining certain attributes as feminine or masculine, but he departs from convention in admiring the androgynous combination of the two. He admired Turgenev for similar reasons, recalling the Russian writer's "magnificent manhood." At the same time, wrote James, Turgenev was "mild" and "soft," with a "singular sweetness. . . . There was an air of neglected strength, as if it had been a part of his modesty never to remind himself that he was strong. He used sometimes to blush like a boy of sixteen" ("Ivan Turgenev," 140).

This condition of the "in-between" has been applied to James himself. According to William Veeder and Susan Griffin, that "Henry James himself combined the feminine and the masculine . . . is readily documented." He was "in-between both psychologically and culturally." His world was not downtown with the men, but "uptown with the women"; not fighting in the Civil War, but looking on; "American by birth, Englishman by volition" (Veeder, 2). James epitomizes the realm of the in-between as an attentive outsider, always observant, often participatory, but never settled. As is said of John Marcher in "The Beast in the Jungle," so might it be said of James that he "had never been settled for an hour in his life" (342). In his wandering between geographical, sexual, and ideological worlds, James shares with several of his fictional creations the peculiar agonies and satisfactions of marginality.

This examination of the margins borrows from several voices both inside and outside James scholarship. As this study deals with the psychology of characters—an issues to which James's text inevitably points—the tone, symbols, and images of Freudian analysis can assist readers in uncovering the psychological twists and turns of the marginal individual fraught with conflicts between self and society. Reference is also made to Michel Foucault's work, including his *History of Sexuality* in order to help locate society's punitive aspect with regard to human sexual behavior—prisons formed whether by concrete, words, or convention to keep the marginal person in line. Foucault's work offers an appropriate reminder of society's boundaries, however much one might prefer to dwell on its seeming openness. In addition to Foucault, Peter Gay's work on Victorian-Edwardian England helps locate sexuality chronologically with specific examples of marginal sexuality at the turn of the century.

Jacques Lacan makes explicit the connection of language and psychology that Freud implied several years earlier. Lacanian vocabulary includes several terms useful in describing the relationship of the marginal individual to language and culture. For Lacan, language is both helpful and harmful to the individual: helpful as it allows the speaker to reap the benefits of a particular culture, harmful as words ultimately serve less the individual speaker than the cultural machine. Roland Barthes's work is helpful in approaching the way marginal characters are talked about and the ways they talk about themselves. Barthes distinguishes healthy language from unhealthy: The healthiest language is self-conscious, always reflecting back on itself in acknowledging the failure of language to adequately express individual aspirations. For Barthes, self-conscious language assists the marginal individual by exposing the cultural biases encoded in words.

Lamentably, little has been written by James scholars on male sexuality and still less has been written on marginal behaviors. Critics appear reluctant to talk openly about the sexual implications of James's work. Even today, many readers avoid the mention of sexuality in James, in part because there is so much uncertainty in his work—if only, so the wish goes, James had clarified for the reader the direction of sexual desire found in those pages, then one might rest easier. On the surface, James's text greets readers with utter conventionality, leading them to take comfort in the supreme respectability of his fiction, never exploring the numerous cracks and crevasses below. For many, James will always be "the Master" writing about the socially acceptable troubles of the upper class, the creator of eloquent phrases and lush metaphors that compose a world of irrefutable decorum.

James is this, and much more—decorous indeed, yet nonetheless inscribing erotic spaces refuted by decorum. In fact, his decorousness raises the terrifying (for some readers) specter of elitism, and hence, effeteness and effeminacy, and hence, aestheticism, decadence, and homoeroticism (Freedman, xv-xvi). Critics who are refreshingly aware of James as a writer of erotic potential include Linda S. Boren in her *Eurydice Reclaimed*, where she discusses the erotic borders of James's fiction, somewhere between decorum and libido. In this marginal zone, she discovers James's attempt to elude censorship through his use of circuitous language. John Carlos Rowe presents a telling discussion of the absent father's power—erotic and otherwise—notably in *The Turn of the Screw*, while David Van Leer and Eve Sedgwick discuss the possibilities of homoeroticism in James's work. Jonathan Freedman in *Professions of Taste* reveals links between James's style and British aestheticism, arguing that New Criticism has concealed James's connection with Pater and other aesthetes because of the potentially ominous undercurrents of voyeurism and homoeroticism. Leon Edel remains the standard source for biography, with additions and revisions from Miranda Seymour's *Ring of Conspirators: Henry James and His Literary Circle*, and Fred Kaplan's *Henry James: The Imagination of Genius, A Biography*.

The purpose of this analysis is to explore the marginal spaces articulated by James. Within what space in language, for example, can the marginal male find his niche? Lambert Strether travels to Europe and finds a world of metaphor that partially frees him from the restrictions of language as he knew it in America. Ralph Touchett in *The Portrait of a Lady* must likewise employ language creatively to defuse the rhetoric of the patriarch, Daniel Touchett, who can say to his son with all the weight of cultural authority behind him that marriage is the right thing to do.

Also, in a world that would deny him pleasure, the man at the margins must scramble for sexual space. James allows characters what might be termed "sexual surprise," pleasure in the moments when it seems that sexuality would be nonexistent. Theirs is the pleasure of disguise, in the form of the nonsexual, assuming the texture of desire only at the margins. Any coded expressions of sexuality become the domain of these men who spend their energies in secret, undetected by society.

James also makes filial accommodations for these marginal figures so like himself. Otherwise trapped in a world not of their own choosing, these characters are temporarily freed from filial obligation by the absence of father figures. Whether on a country estate ruled exclusively by women or on a European voyage beyond the bounds of American Puritanism, these marginal characters enjoy repose from the patriarchal authors of their woes. Indeed the absence of fathers occurs frequently in James's fiction, enough to suggest James's rather negative view of the punitive role of fathers.

In addition, James explores the workings of the imagination, the first and last refuge for the marginal male, asking to what extent a man at the margins can imagine a world of his own creation, modeled not after the aggressive behavior typically associated with masculinity, but upon a nonaggressive model that draws upon the androgynous quality at the core of marginality. It is on the field of the imagination that the battle is fiercest between society and the individual.

James knows the margins from personal experience. Biographical links are numerous in the fiction of a man often ill at ease with the society he knew so well. As much as any of his characters, James exemplifies the person who must know the culture inside and out in order to move beyond it. Conventions do not have any immediate utility for the marginal male who seems to inhabit the patriarchy, all the while watching the culture suspiciously as something not his own. He is on the outside and he knows it. His knowledge is dangerous to himself for it could mean self-loathing and eventual destruction while, on the other hand, it could mean a reassessment of his situation and the creation of some position comparable to the safe world of normative masculinity yet of his own making. What James's work finally catalogs is not an escape from the margins, but a full embrace of that space. The "in-between" character must learn both the limitations and the potential of his peculiar habitat.

1

The Margins

Well into the novel *The Ambassadors*, Lambert Strether wonders what significance, if any, he has in Madame de Vionnet's and Chad Newsome's lives. Has he played nothing more than an adjunct role, rendering him important, as Madame de Vionnet says, only when "we want you"? What Strether faces is the terrifying fact of marginality; whereas he thought himself significant in the lives of his closest friends, he discovers that he is awkwardly other to their sexual intimacy.

Strether's predicament is far from unique in James's work, where many male characters find themselves displaced to the margins of society. An early exploration of this character type appears in *Roderick Hudson*. In this novel, Rowland Mallet, the person through whose eyes the reader views the events, fails to meet the masculine norm because he cannot muster sufficient heterosexual passion for Mary Garland. He is the type in James's work that one critic defines as the "artistic, middle-aged male" who is "unable to act aggressively or sexually" (Przybylowicz, *Desire and Repression*, 4), at least in the manner sanctioned by society. While it appears that he is romantically interested in Mary, this interest is discounted because of his lack of ardor, as he admires her more for her virtue than for her beauty. To him she appears as an anchor against the corrupting forces of Europe. She confesses her distaste for Europe: "If I were to remain here [in Europe], I should . . . become permanently 'low'" (*Roderick Hudson*, 274). Rowland thinks of Mary as a preventative against the moral corruption of his friend Roderick Hudson: "Was it not in itself a guarantee against folly [for Roderick] to be engaged to Mary Garland?" (131).

Rowland's lack of passion for women contrasts with Roderick's ardor. Though Rowland says to Christina Light, "Hudson, as I understand him, does not need, as an artist, the stimulus of strong emotion, of passion" (231), secretly he admires Roderick for the very thing he condemns, a certain abandon to the moment, with intensity and without regret. Rowland admires "the perfect exclusiveness" of Roderick, who never sees himself as part of the whole; only as "the clear-cut, sharp-edged, isolated individual, rejoicing or raging, as the case might be" (325). Rowland envies Roderick his passion, envies him enough in fact to make him desire Roderick in a way that he never desired Mary Garland.

Roderick detects Rowland's lack of passion for women. Late in the novel, he tells Rowland that "there are certain things"—women and what relates to women—"that you know nothing about." Roderick continues, "You have no imagination—no sensibility, nothing to be touched" (373). Rowland considers this "a serious charge"; yet despite his protest, it is undeniable that he fails to pursue women romantically.

On rare occasions Rowland acknowledges his unfortunate position, lamenting to his friend Cecilia early in the novel, "I want to care for something or for somebody. And I want to care with a certain ardor; even, if you can believe it, with a certain passion" (53). Of greater concern to him, however, is the way other people respond to him. Arguably his own lack of passion consigns him to questionable significance in the lives of his so-called friends, who are themselves romantically involved.

In an attempt at significance, Rowland assumes the posture of ambassador, a role that many of James's marginal males share. Rowland's ambassadorship begins, as it does for other ambassadors in James's novels, with a readiness to submit to the will of others; he is vulnerable to exploitation because he lacks an aggressive nature that would promote his own ends. Forced to follow the indirect route to power by means of an "ambassadorship," the marginal male only confirms his marginal status in his awkward attempt at social significance.

James carefully and sympathetically constructs a character who has been consigned early in life to marginal status; Rowland's childhood foretells marginality and raises the question of how much choice this character type has concerning his odd placement in society. As a boy, Rowland lacked the aggression associated with masculinity. His youthful demeanor is described as "passive" and "pliable" (56), and though he was a soldier in the Civil War, he suffered from the thought that his "duty was obscure," with the minor consolation that "on two or three occasions it had been performed with something of an ideal precision" (58). This tendency to disappear into vagueness from early on produces a character ripe for ambassadorship, ready to please.

Rowland agrees to accompany Roderick to Europe in the hope of enhancing the young man's artistic gifts. Mary Garland assigns him the task of watching over Roderick when she asks the older man to make Roderick "do his best" (91), and Rowland hopes to please Mary by pleasing Roderick. Ideally both his friends will recognize the great service he has done them.

Roderick initially accepts Rowland's services, but later he starts to question Rowland's motives, his discontent suggesting an awareness that Rowland expects more from the friendship than the younger man can give. Rowland expects a deep and abiding commitment, whereas Roderick sees the friendship as relatively insignificant, responding simply with the phrase "You have been a great fool to believe in me" (190).

Mary too is incredulous at Rowland's willingness to help out—though she stands to benefit by Rowland's good will, however superficially, she advises Rowland, "You ought at any rate, to do something for yourself" (275). Rowland's shock at this statement demonstrates just how sincere he is about his role as ambassador to other's needs, and how baffled he will be to find out that he lacks any real significance in their lives. He responds, "For myself? I should have supposed that if ever a man seemed to live for himself—." His seeming humility masks his delight in having his generosity confirmed; he relishes the thought that "she has had that speech on her conscience" (275).

His ambassadorial role extends to Christina Light and her in-laws, who expose his vulnerability. Christina's mother tells him outright how momentarily useful but ultimately dispensable he is, explaining to him that the task before him is of the most urgent nature, yet in the same breath remarking that if he fails, "we have something else" (307). His disillusionment foreshadows the much greater psychic wounds that Mary and Roderick will inflict on him. Mary confesses, "If you were to tell me you intended to leave us to-morrow, I am afraid that I should not venture to ask you to stay" (357). Where Rowland once prided himself on a "certain intimacy" (116) with his friends, he now finds superficiality.

Roderick ultimately dismisses Rowland as insignificant in his life, in the hours before his death forcing Rowland to part company with him. Rowland pleads, "I should like to go with you," and Roderick replies, "I am fit only to be alone" (379). Assessing the situation later that day, Rowland considers that despite his "excellent cause," he had been "placed in the wrong" (380). Mary's comment on the situation rings true: "I am afraid your kindness has been a great charge upon you" (356).

Rowland Mallet exemplifies the theme of marginality as it relates to atypical masculine behavior. In James's *Portrait of a Lady*, Ralph Touchett similarly suffers from maladies that block his road to significance in the heterosexual realm. One common reading of the novel is that Ralph does not marry Isabel because he suffers from a lung disorder. Indeed Isabel says, "[Ralph] has a good excuse for his laziness" (*Portrait of a Lady*, 64). However, the problem is more complex than it at first appears. Touchett not only suffers from a physical disability; he also suffers from a lack of desire. Ralph's father, Daniel Touchett, assures his son that he could marry Isabel if he pursued her aggressively. Daniel stands firm on the side of marriage and society, saying to his son, "The best thing you can do, when I'm gone, will be to marry" (156). Ralph protests that he has a bad lung, and adds that it is better not to marry one's cousin; his father, however, maintains his position as guardian of the social norm. Daniel Touchett has the rhetorical advantage, socially sanctioned as the patriarchal voice. He judiciously advises his son not to linger in the margins of bachelorhood, saying with authority, "All you want is to lead a natural life" (157). In Daniel Touchett's view, Ralph's bachelor life carries the taint of incompleteness, as if his son can't live a full life unless he marries. He tells Ralph that he lives on "false principles" (157). To silence his father, Ralph finally denies having any affection for Isabel.

Ralph has earlier admitted to Henrietta Stackpole that he could in fact marry if he chose to do so: "Shall you not believe me to be so on the day I tell you I desire to give up the practice of going round alone?" (85). The word "desire" implies that his object of desire might not be marriage. His failure to tie the heterosexual knot goes beyond physical disabilities and is sufficiently complex to mystify Isabel, who wonders, "What were his views?" (280). Ralph's dilemma raises important questions, for if he is limited not only by ill health, but also by a lack of "normal" passion, then he is emotionally as well as physically unfit for a society that sees as its ultimate goal a person's participation in the rites of marriage.

Unfortunately, Ralph's fondness for bachelorhood may be more costly than he imagines. His affinity for an alternative life relegates him to an ambassadorial role similar to that of Rowland Mallet. At the very moment when his father would have him share the abundant social blessings of marriage with Isabel, Ralph instead crusades for her financial well-being while he remains a bachelor. His payment for such behavior is high: he remains beyond the pale of significance in a heterosexual world.

The costs are apparent in the scene immediately following his encounter with his father on the subject of matrimony. At this point his "amusement" (159) in funding Isabel while never committing himself to marriage consigns him against his will to the status of observer. His lung disorder has worsened, confining him to the house, and instead of enjoying a walk outside with Isabel and her friend Madame Merle, he is forced to watch them from the window. James describes him as "almost a prisoner" (163). In another incident, in Italy, Ralph finds himself once again on the margins of Isabel's life. In what Ralph perceives as emblematic of his exclusion, Isabel withholds from him the details of her marriage. This emotional separation comes as a painful reminder that his disabilities—both physical *and* emotional—have placed Isabel beyond his reach. She is now engulfed in her marriage, with concerns to which a third party cannot be privy.

Ralph falls into the category of the marginalized male because his body *and* his mind fail to meet social expectations. Because he is terminally ill, his virility is in question. But more inciting than the involuntary condition of poor health is his utter lack of desire to marry. With a curiosity bordering on obsession, Daniel puzzles over his son's motives. Abstaining from romance as he does, Ralph's life seems frustratingly to involve and satisfy no one but himself; to a highly successful businessman like Daniel, Ralph's life is nothing but a game. In point of fact, his flaunting of convention masks the serious implications of life at the margins.

Significantly, James portrays his marginal males sympathetically. Something in their experience *compels* these characters to a life outside the norm, and it is in this lack of choice that they attract a large amount of reader sympathy. Further exploration of the sexually marginal male appears in *The Princess Casamassima*, with Hyacinth Robinson as the character incapable of meeting the masculine norm. Besides his poverty and lack of proper education, his appearance connotes impotence. His legs are short, his complexion pale, his hands delicate, his voice high—all suggesting a male less than manly. Unlike his acquaintance Paul Muniment, who appears well-equipped to deal with the rigors placed upon him by society, the small-boned Hyacinth carries the stigma of illness. His deficiency is reinforced in everyday experience, such as his walking through London with the physically and emotionally able Muniment, who asks Hyacinth if he would like to be carried in case his weak limbs fail him (*Princess Casamassima*, 131).

James appears to have anticipated his audience's distaste for Hyacinth's unconventional manhood by describing the horror of Hyacinth's disability in terms similar to his description of the seamy London underworld. Both the environment and the character evoke social ills. Through parallel presentations, Hyacinth's repellent physiognomy becomes emblematic of this underworld. As Mr. Vetch says of the seamier side of life, so the reader might say of the uncomfortable question of Hyacinth's impaired manhood: "[it is] very sad and hideous, and I am happy to say that I soon shall have done with it" (465).

James early on underscores the young man's lack of interest in marriage. If Hyacinth—despite his very feminine-sounding, though classically male, name—were to desire heterosexual romance, then he could find social significance, though Hyacinth "would never marry at all—to that his mind was absolutely made up" (105). The vow against marriage is linked to his disgust with his own male lack, which in turn rests on his inheritance of poverty and ignominy.

Devoid of romantic interest, Hyacinth's association with women takes a unique turn: "If the soft society of women was to be enjoyed on other terms, he should cultivate it with a bold, free mind" (105). Hyacinth looks to the Princess and Millicent not as lovers but as friends, admiring the Princess for her ability to get what she wants, a trait Hyacinth lacks, and admiring Millicent for her strength of simplicity free "from the sophistries of civilisation" (583). His interest in women develops in a way different from romantic passion.

Women find him "theatrical," "exotic," and "wasted," a subject for curiosity and entertainment: they "always found him touching" (105). Madame Poupin tells Hyacinth that she still thinks of him as her "child" (550). The Princess Casamassima finds him curious but stunted. While Hyacinth wishes to be her confidant, the Princess dismisses his words as insignificant, telling Paul Muniment, "He's a dear fellow, with extraordinary qualities, but so deplorably conventional" (500). Much earlier in their relationship, when Hyacinth is staying at the Princess's estate, the Princess infantilizes him by saying, "I wished to leave you free to amuse yourself" (321).

Out of a sense of marginality, Hyacinth longs to be integral to the lives of his closest friends, though by playing the ambassador in bringing Paul Muniment and the Princess together, he loses the intimacy he enjoyed with both. He introduces the two, only to discover that the Princess and Muniment have already met, and he is dismayed by their not needing his introductions. The Princess "had made it to Camberwell without his assistance"; the "feeling that took possession of him was a kind of embarrassment" (406). From then on, he sees them coming and going together, suggesting to him a degree of intimacy he has never experienced: "Hadn't he wanted Paul to know her, months and months before, and now was he to entertain a vile feeling at the first manifestation of an intimacy" (535).

Hyacinth's sense of inadequacy ultimately leads to suicide. He detects the Princess's fondness for a certain aggression in Muniment that he lacks (425). Muniment dismisses Hyacinth as weak and insignificant, and is careless of Hyacinth's risking his life for revolution. Meanwhile the Princess reminds Hyacinth of how much he has been left out of things: "We have information. My dear fellow, you are so much out of it now that if I were to tell you, you wouldn't understand" (575). The effect of these failed personal relationships cannot be underestimated in contributing to his suicide, for Hyacinth thinks just prior to his death "that the Princess had done with him," a thought that "remained the most vivid impression that Hyacinth had carried away from Madeira Crescent that night" (582). On the morning of his suicide, he thought he "had become vague, he was extinct" (582).

In a much later work, Henry James brings to center stage what in earlier works had been textually as well as socially marginalized. Lambert Strether in *The Ambassadors* (1903) offers the most complete illustration of James's marginal male. Prior to this novel, marginal males were cast in marginal roles, appearing now and again at the service of more central characters, with Rowland Mallet as confidant to Roderick Hudson, and Ralph Touchett illuminating Isabel Archer. And while Hyacinth Robinson is the central character of *The Princess Casamassima*, James distracts the reader by naming the novel after the Princess. In addition, these earlier examples precede the consciously dramatic style of James's later work, interrupting the marginal point of view with more conventional perspectives. Not until *The Ambassadors* does James assign an exclusive point of view, main character status, and title of the novel to the marginal male; in this novel, the "fine alienated sensibility would be the central sensibility in James" (Habegger, *Gender* 291).

Lambert Strether epitomizes James's marginal male. The death of his family erases his connection with marriage, bringing to bear the "multiple pressures of erasure that threaten people of marginal existence" (Yingling, *Hart Crane*, 36). In the company of Maria Gostrey, Strether is surprised at the thought that he is finally dining with a woman after the "grey middle desert" of the years between the death of his wife and that of his son, thinking that his dining with a woman before accompanying her to a play has "never before—no literally never" (*Ambassadors*, 43) involved him; he has missed out not only on what might have been, but also on what should have been in terms of social acceptability. His first marriage lacked the elements of romance that a man might expect to enjoy: "He had married, in the far-away years, so young as to have missed the time natural in Boston for taking girls to the Museum" (43).

The vagueness of Strether's desire, like the vagueness Hyacinth Robinson discovers, frustrates easy analysis. He comes to Paris supposedly to perform a simple task, ultimately in the service of marriage. However, his goal of marrying Mrs. Newsome blends with other desires that enmesh and finally consume it. One is the desire for money: Strether's lack of financial success in a capitalistic world calls attention to his lack of aggression, and therefore of masculinity. His situation can be compared with that of Waymarsh, who has on his side the "fine silence" of a socially sanctioned separation from his wife; he has done what any "man" would do—desert an unsuitable wife, in the bargain attaining enviable status: he "had held his tongue and had made a large income; and these were in especial the achievements as to which Strether envied him" (31).

Both Waymarsh and Strether have their secrets, but Strether's secret is, embarrassingly, a financial one. He "had indeed on his side too a subject for silence, which he fully appreciated; but it was a matter of a different sort, and the figure of the income he had arrived at had never been high enough to look any one in the face" (31). The connection between the world of finances and sex is nothing new in James's fiction by the time of his writing *The Ambassadors*, but it assumes a unique subtlety here in terms of masculinity. Here, a lack of success in the business world reveals a character's lack as well in areas of romance.

This intertwining of finances and sexuality develops in a scene where Strether is dining with Maria Gostrey and notices a velvet ribbon in her hair. Instead of permitting himself a moment's appreciation of his companion's accessory, he catches himself, calling attention to his financial and sexual inadequacies and linking the two inextricably. Strether is troubled by his precarious place in the world of men, a world that demands devotion to work and money, not to trivialities like a woman's velvet band. His lack of success in the business world, he feels, denies him the right to romantic fulfillment.

Pushed to the margins by his financial failure, Strether is also suspect in another way, uncertain as he is about the focus of his sexual desire. One might assume that he wants to remarry, inasmuch as he is courting Mrs. Newsome. However, any romantic impulse on his part mingles inextricably with his need for money. As Waymarsh says, "You'll marry—you personally—more money" (75). Strether's desires are complicated further by his strong attraction to Chad, the very person he intended to convert to the ways of Woollett. He adores "Chad's easiest urbanity" (141), finding Chad's social skills intimately tied to masculinity and power and therefore to personal freedom, admiring in this "irreducible young pagan" (99) what he himself does not possess—power, virility, and unquestioned masculinity.

Rather than censuring the young American, Strether admires Chad's extramarital romance. The young man seems to succeed in confirming his virility because of, not in spite of, his flaunting of social convention. Bilham explains to Strether that Chad operates from a sense of power rather than morality: "He wants to be free. He isn't used, you see," says little Bilham, "to being so good" (112). Far from rejecting him as immoral, Strether admires the almost animal-like Chad—on a near primal level. "It made him admire..., made him envy, the glossy male tiger, magnificently marked" (133). Strether's "stirred sense" now focuses on the male, skewing the reader's sense of Strether's maleness. Chad remains secure in his masculinity, while Strether envies what he does not have.

James adds to the theme of marginality Strether's failure as an artist. Strether thinks of the *Woollett Review*, which he "not at all magnificently" edits (50). He is "really rather disappointed" that Maria Gostrey hasn't heard of the publication. Only the thought of the journal's green cover inscribed with his name restores his self-confidence. These superficial details—cover and name—symbolize his marginal significance in society; to Mrs. Newsome, he is momentarily useful, but always dispensable. She offers Strether the place of authorship only as part of a contract that includes the promise of financial well-being for Strether but with innumerable conditions attached—Mrs. Newsome controls all the strings.

Strether's role as ambassador parallels in several ways the roles played by other of James's sexually marginal males. Strether is suited to the role of ambassador because he is passive. His vulnerability stems in part from his gregariousness, a highly attractive aspect of his character. His verbosity contrasts with the silence of types like Waymarsh who remain in positions of power by withholding themselves, whereas Strether surrenders himself at every turn. Also, his painful shyness (37) prepares him to be used by others, so he resigns himself to being used by Mrs. Newsome in her efforts to uncover the activities of her son, Chad, in Europe.

Strether mistakenly believes that his ambassadorship for Mrs. Newsome will secure him a permanent niche in society's power structure, imagining therefore that his task is enormously significant: "If I'm squared where's my marriage? If I miss my errand I miss that; and if I miss that I miss everything—I'm nowhere" (75). His desire to serve and be significant makes him extend his ambassadorship to assist Madame de Vionnet and Chad. He hopes to serve others in order to achieve significance in their lives.

What Strether retains through much of the novel is the confidence that, if committed to his tasks, he will benefit both himself and those he serves. "No one could explain better when needful, nor put more conscience into an account or a report" (92). He does not think of himself as exploited, for he expects the rewards to justify his efforts. His naiveté adds to his sympathetic portrayal. Other characters, meanwhile, are incredulous at his willingness to be so used. Chad says, "What I don't for the life of me make out is what you *gain* by it" (290). Maria Gostrey meanwhile questions his serving Madame de Vionnet and Chad: "If your idea's to stay [in Paris] for them you may be left in the lurch" (295).

His confidence in his own ability, and his confidence in others to reward him with their friendship, never wavers until the climax of the novel, when he sees Madame de Vionnet and Chad in a moment of intimacy. Upon discovering them on the river, what horrifies him is not simply the affront to his Puritanism.[1] Rather what arrests him is a consciousness of the very small role he plays in their lives: his concern at the novel's climax is for self-esteem as he makes the shocking discovery that he sits in the darkness of insignificance while others enjoy the warmth of intimacy. Strether acknowledges that the fact of intimacy between two people leaves the third party "lonely and cold." "That was what, in his vain vigil, he oftenest reverted to: intimacy, at such a point, was *like* that—and what in the world else would one have wished it to be like?" (313). Madame de Vionnet and Chad represent the heterosexual union to which the sexually marginalized male comes unprepared physically and emotionally.

Strether's marginality in playing the ambassador illustrates the dichotomy between the illusions held by the marginal figure and the incapability of society to finally accommodate that person. In Lambert Strether, James creates a sympathetic character who stands to inherit very little, the reason being that marriage is the clarion call of a heterosexual society. What places Strether even more in the margins is that, despite his original attachment to Mrs. Newsome, he questions the very basis of marriage. The specter of the affable, bumbling Jim Pocock haunts Strether. Pocock is a man who has married and so secured a place in Woollett but who has also been swallowed up by marriage to the point of losing his identity: "Pocock was normally and consentingly though not quite wittingly out of the question" (213). Strether calls him "Mrs. Jim," and views him as emasculated by the institution that supposedly assures the man power. Whether or not Jim suffers from this state—and there is ample verification of Strether's view—Strether feels that he might suffer the same plight.

Seen from a different perspective, Jim has fared better than Strether in terms of the masculine norm, managing to please society by associating with women on a romantic level. In contrast, Strether associates with women on a purely social basis; they are his best friends. In this way, Strether enjoys "an odd situation for a man" (213). Marriage would cost him the friendships he now enjoys with women: "It kept coming back to him in a whimsical way that he should find his marriage had cost him his place" (213). However, in his present state as a sexually inactive bachelor, he actually suffers far more at least in terms of his identity as a man.

The question of his filling the quotient of masculinity bothers Strether, and his friends unwittingly reinforce his sense of inadequacy. Madame de Vionnet, for example, asks if he isn't "a man in trouble" (177). Strether construes this query as an attack on his manhood: "He felt himself colour at the question, and then hated that—hated to pass for anything so idiotic as woundable" (177). His response suggests that his male identity is the aspect of his personality most easily wounded.

Lambert Strether and the other aforementioned characters hold at best a precarious, and by some views reprehensible, position in society. That they should be sympathetically drawn suggests that they share a commonality with their creator. Indeed Henry James's life can in many aspects be seen as a study in marginality, one that would offer rich resources on which the author might draw for the unique male characters in his fiction. It takes little imagination to view James's life as correlative to the existence of his marginal male characters. Biography may help to pinpoint more precisely where this marginal type stands in relation to society.

A key issue in both Henry James's life and the lives of his fictional characters is that of *choice*. How much choice did James have in the life he led? There is a need to reexamine James's life in order to trace the pattern of marginality that contradicts the notion that James freely chose his "life of the imagination." His "choice" of renunciation may in fact rest on a quality of marginality that shaped his life while informing his work with the subtle type of the timid male whose timidity rests not so much on choices made as on choices made for him by a society oriented toward a single norm of sexuality and masculinity.

The catalog of James's marginal status is a lengthy one, at every step reinforcing a general condition of exclusion from the norm. Like the marginal males in his fiction, James exhibited a reluctance to marry, a fact troubling to a society that would have him conclude his bachelorhood. One cause for gossip was James's friendship with Emilie Grigsby, a wealthy Kentuckian who saw James as her ticket into the British literati. Her method of securing ties with James was to spread the false notion that he wished to marry her. In a letter rushed off to his brother William, Henry shows his determination to rout any suspicion about an impending marriage, signing the letter, "Your hopelessly celibate even though sexegenarian Henry" (Seymour, *A Ring of Conspirators*, 102). James felt compelled to allay society's suspicions on the subject of his marriage.

On occasion James envied the security of married life. In a letter to William and his wife, Alice, he wrote, "How large your life swings compared to mine, and how much—beside the lone bachelor's—it takes in!" (*Letters*, 4:5).[2] It is not so much the actuality of his bachelorhood that might well concern the James scholar, but rather James's imaginative concept of it. He acknowledged his freedom but felt himself on the margins of life because of an essential loneliness. His bachelorhood warded off society, but at a price. In a revealing letter to Morton Fullerton, James answered his friend's question about what "port" James sailed from. He wrote, "The port from which I set out was, I think, that of the *essential loneliness of my life*—and it seems to be the port also, in sooth to which my course again finally directs itself! This loneliness, (since I mention it!)—what is it still but the deepest thing about one? Deeper about *me*, at any rate, than anything else" (*Letters*, 4:170). These words convey, in a moment of truthful surrender, his life course as he perceived it: not one of centrality, but one of marginality. His bachelor state contributed to the sense that other people were participating in social privileges that were denied him; marriage represented to him the epicenter of society, a "type of belonging" that was "incompatible with his needs" (Kaplan, *Henry James*, 34). To marry meant to submit to what society held up as life, something James refused to do.

Another aspect of James's marginality is his relationship with his older brother William. William might well be viewed in light of the Lacanian concept of the "other" (Rowe, *Theoretical Dimensions*, 104),[3] a source of endless conflict for Henry. Oddly enough, the younger brother cherished this problematic relationship to the point of obsession. In his essay "Henry James: Interpreting an Obsessive Memory," Richard Hall conjectures that Henry James was fixated on his brother. Leon Edel finds resonance in Hall's remarks: "Once we agree [with Hall] on Henry's love fixation on William, that explains a lot of things" (Hall, "Interpreting," 85). Edel's agreement with Hall raises the question of why Edel dealt with the possibility of Henry's fixation so little in his biography.[4] Edel wrote to Hall, "If I were writing these volumes today I would indeed make much more of this" (Hall, "Interpreting," 84). Edel's bypassing of this possibility in his biography mirrors the response of many of James's readers who find little significance in details that heighten the sense of James as marginal, particularly sexually marginal. Nonetheless, reports of James's life by his friends Edmund Gosse and Hugh Walpole take the issue of marginality beyond conjecture.

Gosse and Walpole reveal James in a rare moment of candor concerning his private life. In a telling comment about James, Gosse recorded in his *Aspects and Impressions* (1922), "There had hung over him a sort of canopy, a mixture of reserve and deprecation, faintly darkening the fullness of communion with his character; there had always been something indefinably non-conductive between him and those in whom he had most confidence." Gosse then relates one particular occasion, at twilight on a summer evening, when he and James were walking in the gardens at Rye. According to Gosse's account, James suddenly began talking in a "profuse and enigmatic language," recounting a strange event from his past. Gosse writes,

> James spoke of standing on the pavement of a city, in the dusk, and of gazing upwards across the street, watching, watching for the lighting of a lamp on the third storey. And the lamp blazed out, and through bursting tears he strained to see what was behind it, the unapproachable face. And for hours he stood there, wet with the rain, brushed by the phantom figures of the scene, and never from behind the lamp was for one moment visible the face. (Gosse, *Aspects and Impressions*, 42-43)[5]

Gosse writes that after the story both he and James stood in absolute silence, unable to make conversation, after which James suddenly disappeared into the house for an hour.

This commentary provides several parallels between James and those male characters in his fiction who find themselves sexually marginalized. Most significantly, the reader is confronted here by a desired object, which Hall assumes is Henry's brother William. Hall goes a long way in proving this assumption, recalling that this event in James's "obsessive memory" must have occurred while he was traveling with his brother in Europe.

Perhaps more significant than the possibility of Henry's infatuation with William is the unattainability of the desired object, whatever that object might have been. James could not see the face at the window, and were the face to appear, desire would have been sustained because of the physical space separating subject and object. Hall labels this scenario "window straining," which he finds applicable to numerous situations in James's fiction where the act of "sexual exclusion" occurs (Hall, "Interpreting," 94). Hall's concept of exclusion could well be applied to the marginal male who is excluded from social acceptance because his sexual wishes are the taboos of the status quo. Did such a "window straining" scene actually occur? Hugh Walpole, in *The Horizon*, corroborates Gosse's account: "Sexually also he [James] had suffered some frustration. What that frustration was I never knew, but I remember him telling me how he had once in his youth in a foreign town watched a whole night in pouring rain for the appearance of a figure at the window. That was the end . . .' he said, and broke off" (quoted in Hall, "Interpreting," 88). Again, the writings that Hall brings to light are intriguing, not because they verify James's sexual activity (if any existed), but because they verify a psychological state that persists in his fiction—that of the unattainability of the desired object. As for the "window episode," whether or not the incident occurred, James's "obsessive memory" of it creates the scenario for what happens to James's fictional characters who strain after objects that elude them. As James said of Lambert Strether in his introduction to *The Ambassadors*, Strether's "very groping would figure among his most interesting motions" (*Ambassadors*, 9).[6]

Another aspect of James's marginality was his apparent passivity. His "obscure hurt" exemplifies his sense of impairment, whether physical or psychological. This self-definition encouraged passivity, as opposed to the more active and stereotypically masculine role that his brother William assumed. Henry played a passive role in the Civil War; his father refused him active participation (Seymour, 268). More than one biographer has argued that James was taught from an early age to be submissive, while his older brother favored an active role (Seymour, 70).[7] William set out on personal voyages, soon to be followed by Henry, who found himself outdone, whether in grade school or at the university (Edel, *Henry James*, 1:61-62). Years later Henry described their situation as one where "what I probably most did, all the while, was but to pick up, and to the effect not a bit of starving but quite of filling myself, the crumbs of his [William's] feast and the echoes of his life" (*Notes of a Son and Brother*, 12).[8] On one of his visits to London, William observed his younger brother's essential "powerlessness" in all respects save in his art (Seymour, 127). By proclaiming his brother's passivity, William reinforced the role he demanded of Henry. In truth, Henry's passivity surfaced largely when he was in William's company, as if Henry sought to confirm William's analysis of him as powerless (Seymour, 127). While William and Henry related to one another "intellectually as adults, emotionally they were still back in Fourteenth Street, in the 1850s" (Edel, 5:322).[9]

The uncertainty that James felt about his ability to assert himself against the world spilled over into other aspects of his life. His art was threatened by William's persistent reminder that Henry was the younger, and therefore more submissive, sibling. William frequently chastised Henry for his circuitous method of writing. The elder brother had long encouraged his younger brother to go into something more practical than art, and now that Henry was involved in fiction, the least he could do would be to forthrightly reveal his themes and characters instead of skirting the issues.

William's biting criticism accompanied even the later novels. Henry had sent his brother a copy of *The Golden Bowl*, hoping for some encouragement, and instead received word that the book had gone against all of William's notions of how a book should be written. William wrote, "Why don't you, just to please Brother, sit down and write a new book, with no twilight or mustiness in the plot, with great vigour and decisiveness in the action, no fencing in the dialogue, or psychological commentaries, and absolute straightness of style" (quoted in Edel, 5:300). William oddly enough demanded more assertion from Henry in his fiction, whereas in life William permitted no such assertive behavior from him.

Negative responses to Henry's artistic endeavors did not end with William. A less-than-affirmative response from many of his friends to such books as *The American Scene* would only reinforce William's condemnation of Henry's work. The public never responded adequately to Henry's need for approval either. He would always feel inferior from a lack of the same popular acclaim so readily given to several of his contemporaries, including Edith Wharton and H. G. Wells.

Thus while critics would rave about his work, his popular significance was slight. James worked hard at, and was particularly satisfied with, *The Ambassadors*. He no doubt anticipated big sales but was to see small figures in contrast to those garnered by his good friend H. G. Wells, to whom he wrote, "My book has been out upwards of a month, and, not emulating your 4,000, has sold, I believe, to the extent of 4 copies. In America it is doing better—

promises to reach 400" (quoted in Seymour, 92). Wells churned out books rapidly, while James saw only minor profits after comparatively long labors. This contrast with another's success would repeat itself with Edith Wharton, who enjoyed astounding sales. *The House of Mirth* earned its author some $20,000 in 1905, and in 1906 became the best-selling novel of any American work of fiction, selling more than 100,000 copies (Seymour, 237). In a humorous anecdote now famous among James scholars, Henry James quipped that while Edith Wharton had purchased a new Packard automobile with the proceeds from her popular success *The Valley of Decision*, he had with his proceeds from *The Wings of the Dove* "purchased a small go-cart, or hand-barrow, on which my guest's luggage is wheeled from the station to my house." He continued, "It needs a coat of paint. With the proceeds of my next novel I shall have it painted" (quoted in Seymour, 237).

James was never better than in these moments of humor at masking his private lament that artistic success failed to pay adequate dividends. His reward was one which satisfied his ideal, but left him wanting in the ways society-at-large judged success. His dilemma sometimes surfaced in the baldest fashion, revealing his need for significance in all the ways anticipated by a "successful" artist. He is reported to have said to one successful writer of his time, "You are popular! Your admirable work is appreciated by a wide circle of readers; it has achieved popularity. Mine—never goes into a second edition. I should so much have loved to be popular" (quoted in Seymour, 236).

Two incidents highlighted his need for public acclaim, acclaim that would have assuaged his feelings of marginality. An early devastation occurred with the failure of his stage play *Guy Domville*. On the unfortunate night of the play's performance, James chose not to attend his own play, but went instead to a production of Oscar Wilde's *An Ideal Husband*. While the highly popular Oscar Wilde increased in popularity, James's play was booed out of the theater. When the last line went out: "I'm the *last*, my lord, of the Domvilles!" someone in the audience jeered, "It's a bloody good thing y'are" (quoted in Edel, 4:78). Where he had sought to master the situation, the situation had instead mastered him—a reminder of his powerlessness to assert himself in society. The failure sent him into one of the gloomiest periods on record, what he called "The most horrible hours of my life" (quoted in Edel, 4:84). James said after enduring his dark night of the soul, "It has been a great relief that one of the most detestable incidents of my life has closed" (quoted in Edel, 4:88).

In fact, such failure became familiar to James and would foreshadow the failure surrounding the publication of the New York edition of his reprinted novels (1907-1910), after which Edith Wharton recalled how changed James was from the man "so completely the master of his wonderful emotional instrument." She writes, "I could hardly believe it was the same James who cried out to me his fear, his despair, his craving for the cessation of consciousness, & all his unspeakable loneliness & need of comfort, & inability to be comforted" (Seymour, 123). While James had anticipated the New York edition to be the crowning achievement of his later years, the editions sold at an astonishingly low rate. His first royalty would total only $211 (*Letters*, 4:498). His response was emotional breakdown. At his breakdown, he collected his private papers, including forty years of letters, manuscripts, and notebooks, heaped them up, and burned them (Edel, 5:437). Concerning the breakdown, James's nephew Harry wrote,

> There was nothing for me to do but to sit by his side and hold his hand while he panted and sobbed for two hours until the Doctor arrived, and stammered in despair so eloquently and pathetically that as I write of it, the tears flow down my cheeks again. He talked about Aunt Alice and his own end and I knew him to be facing not only the frustration of all hopes and ambitions, but the vision looming close and threatening to his weary eyes, of a lingering illness such as hers. In sight of all that, he wanted to die. . . . He didn't have a good night and the next day the same thing began again with a fear of being alone. (quoted in Edel, 5:440)

Still other factors affected his precarious stance in society. After the failure of his play, Henry wrote to William, "Oscar Wilde's farce which followed *Guy Domville* is, I believe, a great success—and with his two roaring successes running now at once he must be raking in the profits" (quoted in Edel, 4:88). Such a commentary allows a connection to be made between his felt lack of social significance as an artist and his felt failure to perform in a "manly" fashion in another arena—the world of business. He was to say to Howells, who had just aided him in the book trade in America, that he felt, in his ineptitude in business matters, "like an old maid against the wall and on her lonely bench" (quoted in Edel, 4:199). In this phrase, James metaphorically linked a lack of business sense with a sexual lack, cognizant as he was of the shame of a man who lacked skill with finances.

While James always had money, there was never quite enough in comparison with his peers. From early on James knew the pressure of the "silver cord" that bound him first to his parents for aid, and then to his older brother. One example of that financial dependency came when James decided to purchase Lamb House. Though he owned capital, he had very little money on hand to make the purchase. He wrote to his brother William (who handled all his financial affairs) intending to request money, but feeling also the need to justify his expenses. He wrote, "Don't be alarmed. . . . I don't mean that I've received a proposal of marriage" (quoted in Edel, 4:318). The realm of finances, so crucial in James's time and place, mingled with the other elements of self-doubt that threatened his sense of self. William condemned his brother's decision as "extravagant." Henry went ahead and purchased the house anyway, in one of his few assertive acts against William. His desperation over assuming control of his own life had reached a crisis when he wrote,

> My whole being cries out loud for something I can call my own—and when I look round me at the splendour of so many of the 'literary' fry, . . . and I feel that I may strike the world as still, at 56, with my long labour and my genius, reckless, presumptuous and unwarranted in curling up (for my more assured peaceful production) in a poor little $10,000 shelter—once and for all and for all time—*then* I do feel the bitterness of humiliation, the iron enters into my soul, and (I blush to confess it,) I *weep!* But enough, enough, enough! (quoted in Edel, 319-320)

His financial woes continued to haunt him. Edith Wharton served as one constant reminder of the wealth of America that had not been his (*Letters*, 4:xxi), her vast wealth at The Mount from across the Atlantic providing stark contrast to James's Lamb House, where he described his situation as beggarly (*Letters*, 4:352). Indeed his house might appear grand to modern day viewers, but the important issue is one of perceived difference: how James interpreted his financial situation in relation to the wealth of his peers. Money was by no means a taboo subject to James; he would often joke about his situation, to the point that Edith Wharton decided to raise a substantial gift in his behalf. When his nephew Harry informed him of Wharton's scheme, James was outraged: "A more reckless and indiscreet undertaking, with no ghost of a preliminary leave asked, no hint of a sounding taken, I cannot possibly conceive—and am still rubbing my eyes for incredulity" (quoted in Edel,

5:484). The thought of being pitied horrified him. His extreme response—
his anger and sense of insult—suggests that money pointed to deeper
insecurities. He could not abide public notice of his financial need, which he
felt might lead to doubts about his "performance" in other areas. James never
apologized for his denouncement of Wharton's efforts on his behalf.

Another issue that touches on the lives of both the author and his marginal
male characters is their frequent participation in ambassadorial roles, acting
in behalf of others, and in that sense being essentially passive as they act
without immediate self-aggrandizement. James was in demand as a confidant
and character witness in the affairs of his heterosexually active friends. Violet
Hunt looked to James as an "ambassador" in her relationship with Ford Madox
Hueffer, finding in James the perfect gentleman to represent Hueffer and
herself in their divorce trials. James had corresponded with Hunt for some
time and had already invited her to stay at Lamb House when news of the
pending divorce proceedings reached him. At this point, Hunt solicited
James as an ally for her cause. He flatly refused, realizing the possible effects
of his implication, prizing as he did his good name. What stands out in this
scenario is that he would indeed have been the perfect ally, unmarried and
unimplicated in any romantic relationship of his own, available for the whims
of a heterosexually linked couple.

Edith Wharton likewise looked to James as an ambassador in her relationship with Morton Fullerton, both to bring them together and to assist them
in divorces from earlier marriages. As in the situation with Hunt, James
represented to Wharton a perfect ally and confidant but, as was not the case
with Violet Hunt, James felt a genuine fondness for Wharton. He depended
upon her for professional counsel, and as a source of leisure par excellence
at her Massachusetts estate, The Mount.

As for Morton Fullerton, the young man held an attraction both physical
and intellectual for the author. James met Fullerton in the 1880s, and ever
after found him to be appealing company, enough so to confess to him his
essential loneliness along with other dissatisfactions of his life. Consequently, James found no shame in introducing Fullerton and Wharton to each
other, never displaying a hint of suspicion that the two might become lovers.
After all, Wharton was married and Fullerton had not advertised his frequent
and incessant romances. It was with great surprise that James found himself
then operating as a go-between, now finding himself important mostly as a

listening ear. James didn't discover the fact of their intimacy until Wharton confided in him out of a need for consolation, whereupon he advised her in a now famous statement, not unlike the unattached Strether to the younger Bilham, to "Sit tight yourself and *go through the movements of life*, live it all through every inch of it . . . waitingly" (quoted in Edel, 5:413).

James found himself suddenly embroiled in a torrid affair complicated by previous entanglements on both sides. As difficult as the situation was, more painful to him was the fact that neither party had informed him of the particulars of their relationship earlier, which made him feel left out. James couldn't help wishing in particular that Fullerton had confided in him more: "I think of the whole long mistaken perversity of your averted *reality* so to speak, as a miserable *personal* waste, that of something—ah, so tender!—in *me* that was only quite yearningly ready for you, and something all possible, and all deeply and admirably appealing in yourself, of which I never got the benefit" (quoted in Edel, 5:416).

Fullerton confided in James only to ask advice about how to escape his previous relationship. Wharton too begged from James some advice on how to extricate herself from an intolerable marriage. James felt jealousy as much as anything else at having been left out for so long (Seymour, 246); nonetheless, he gave advice and also provided the cover for financial aid to Fullerton in the form of a commission from Macmillan Publishing for Fullerton to write a book. James, it would seem, had a hand in every pie, until he finally conceded that the duties had indeed been greater than the rewards. Such a concession comes more or less in his saying to Wharton that it was she who had "saved" Fullerton in the end, and not he. In this statement, James admits society's valuing of lover over friend.

Such marginality shows James at the mercy of circumstance. While he has been hailed as the writer of fiction who depicts characters supremely equipped to make choices with their wealth and education, his own life shows a striking susceptibility to psychological, physical, and social forces. It is hardly accidental, then, that James's fiction includes many characters who share this precarious relationship to the social norm. The implication of this view is that James and his work detail an enormous interest in the limitations of society and the need for psychological space for such misfit individuals.

A review of the catalog of James's marginal situations suggests that his fiction served as an imaginative stimulus for the creation of marginal male characters in his fiction; "his otherness would become a crucial element in his art" (Kaplan, 36). By writing fiction about these nonheroes, James would raise the question, How can such marginal figures find self-expression, comfort, and space in a closed society? The tracing of marginality answers these questions while exposing James's fictional world as startlingly unconventional.

2

Private Fictions

Henry James celebrated the powers of the imagination, which he felt helped a person to appreciate worlds and lives different from his or her own, noting also that the imagination protected a person from excessive self-confrontation. For James, life is fiction. In a letter to H. G. Wells, dated 10 July 1915, he wrote, "It is art that *makes* life, makes interest, makes importance . . . and I know of no substitute whatever for the force and beauty of its process" (*Letters*, 4:770). Carren Kaston interprets this often-quoted comment as evidence of James's conviction that "living is itself an authorial act." She conjectures that, in James's view, life "consists of competing authorial designs: each character tries to possess the material of life in a version of his or her own making." Individuals' lives are most their own when they live their own fictions rather than when they are forced to "live a fiction invented by some other author" (Kaston, *Imagination*, 6).

The underlying assumption is that fictions about life are inevitable and thereby normal and healthy. Indeed, there is ample evidence to suggest that James welcomed such fictions as part of his own life. He wrote about his childhood, "What happened all the while, I conceive, was that I imagined things . . . wholly other than as they were, and so carried on in the midst of the actual ones an existence that somehow floated and saved me."

James's interest in re-inscribing reality on his own terms is suggested by his fondness for rewriting the lives of those around him. Leon Edel provides evidence that James "freely altered" the letters of his brother and father in *Notes on a Son and Brother* (Edel, 1:60-61). And in the case of Minnie Temple, James altered his young cousin's letters to better suit her past life to his present condition. In this re-inscription, Edel contends that James's motives were more interior than exterior (Edel, 1:61), for in his alteration of the letters he imaginatively rewrote *his* place in their lives. The web of subordination and dependency he imagined in his relationship with a father, a brother, or a cousin could be affirmed or denied as he wished.

It is this self-reflective use of the imagination that most applies to a study of Henry James and his marginal male characters, for turned inward, the imagination can protect the self from a self-image that might prove destructive. As has been discussed in the previous chapter, the marginal male is at pains to see himself as central in a society that persistently devalues him. Relations with women, with men, with health and financial well-being—all create negative images about the male self that, when taken collectively, invite an emotional crisis such that it would seem imperative that some psychological mechanism be set up to protect the subject from internalizing this sense of worthlessness.

James watched a man seemingly secure in his position in society suffer an identity crisis: he witnessed the near psychological dissolution his father during the elder James's "vastation." Henry James, Sr., wrote, "The thing had not lasted ten seconds before I felt myself a wreck; that is, reduced from a state of firm, vigorous, joyful manhood to one of almost helpless infancy." What threatened the elder James? Edel writes, "A deathly presence thus unseen had stalked from his mind into the house" (Edel, 1:30). It was not an external cause, but some terror from within.[1]

Evidence exists that the younger Henry James was concerned about the security of his own identity. James's nephew reported that "Uncle H. has a very lively consciousness of his father's vacillations and impulses . . .often realized to the disturbance of his equanimity" (Edel, 1:138). What is curious here is the corollary that the younger Henry drew between his father's disturbance and his own well-being, perhaps seeing in himself the fragility of identity that marked his father, and consequently marshalling the powers of the imagination to affirm a sense of self otherwise maligned by self-doubt. When the reality of life in the James family became too much to bear, Henry would make himself "small and quiet among the other Jameses," and turn "into the depths of himself to fashion a fictional world" (Edel, 1:66). One has only to read the first few pages of *Notes of a Son and Brother*, describing James's education in Europe, to discover just how vivid were the young Henry's private "impressions" of the world and his place in it. In this memoir, James recalls how his childhood imagination altered time and place to accommodate the self: "They had begun, the impressions—that was what was the matter with them—to scratch quite audibly at the door of liberation, of extension, of projection. . . . Impressions were not merely all right but were the dearest things in the world; only one would have gone to the stake rather than in the first place confessed to some of them, or in the second announced that one really lived by them and built on them" (*Notes of a Son and Brother*, 24).

Jacques Lacan discusses the realm of the imagination as it relates to the child and the child's place in society. In Lacanian terms, when a child learns to speak, he becomes fragmented, subjected to words that inherently fail to describe what he thinks and feels. In contrast, the child's realm before language is imagined by the child as whole and indestructible, what Lacan calls the realm of the *imaginary*. This early childhood phase is also called "mirroring," so named for the moment when the child first looks in the mirror and sees a whole image of the self, at this precise moment viewing himself as completely secure, connected at every limb. This "jubilant assumption" of the child's "specular image" produces a surge of power so pleasing that the child will seek that sensation time and again (Lacan, *Ecrits*, 2).

Once the child experiences fragmentation through the acquisition of a culturally borrowed language, the gaze in the mirror is rendered false insofar as it denies the reality of fragmentation. Even as an adult, the subject will fondle pleasing self-images that recall a wholeness felt in early childhood (Lacan, 2). Lacan adopts the term *imago*, defined as any one of a number of false images created by the ego to which the ego returns to reaffirm its accepted sense of self. Imagos are those dominant "phantoms" that form "the statue in which man projects himself" (Lacan, 3), steering the ego in a "fictional direction, which will always remain irreducible for the individual alone" (Lacan, 2). Because the subject views the world through the false lens of imagos, the resulting picture of externality is often distorted, being the product of misconception, or *méconnaissance* (Lacan, 15).

By calling these fictions of the self "false" and the source of *méconnaissance*, one risks perceiving them as negative. However, suppose the environment in which the subject finds himself is itself false, bombarding the individual with a communal "bad faith." Imagine a society that has condemned the individual to a communal fiction altogether at odds with the individual's sense of self.[2] James and his marginal male characters battle with fictions created by a culture that in "bad faith" denies variant texts of manhood to which James and his marginal males could comfortably subscribe. In the sense described by Julia Kristeva, perhaps a marginal male could compose his own fiction from his imaginary world, in "a transgression of the symbolic order" imposed by society (Kristeva, *Kristeva Reader*, 115).

Henry James engaged in a complex dialogue with society on the subject of masculinity. On the one hand, James abhorred flagrant violations of convention—Oscar Wilde's public displays repulsed him—and was by no means a revolutionary in the sense of wishing radical social change. On the other hand, James demonstrated a persistent and expanding awareness of the unfairness of society toward marginal figures like himself. Time and again, in literature and in life, James favored the subtle alteration of culture to accommodate difference; his mission was not to obliterate the fiction written by society, but to write himself into its pages.

James learned early the value of accommodation in revolution. While masculinity taught one to fight openly against oppression, James sought superficial accommodation to appease authority figures like his father and brother. On his travels abroad as a young man, he learned to satisfy these authority figures by retreating into a mode of powerlessness, indeed to see himself as small and powerless. As Fred Kaplan argues, "Powerlessness [for James] has its attraction" (Kaplan, *Henry James*, 33). This odd mixture of freedom and submission became a lifelong formula for survival on the part of James, an alternative to the naked action and aggression of his beloved rival and elder brother. William James "from the beginning . . . expressed himself more articulately, more assertively, more dramatically. He made family drama. He did his work in public. . . . He took up visible space, a dominant presence" (Kaplan, 33-34). While William followed the path of least resistance in the pose of conventional masculinity, Henry, it could be argued, fought the greater battle by creating an alternative male position of immediate accommodation with partial but long-term disentanglement from entrenched codes of masculinity.

Kaplan employs the image of the cage to describe Henry James's superficial submission to authority, a cage that allowed him a place "without any restrictions on his feelings and thoughts." Within the codes of decorum established by family and society, James nurtured the inner self. "Rebellion would be unseemly, churlish, ungrateful, perhaps even hurtful" (Kaplan, 33). The cage of friends and family allowed him to be cared for and left alone, partly to nurture the fantastic visions he had of himself that bore little resemblance to reality. As a child, James had little restraint in wandering far from reality in the images of his mind, cherishing, for example, the image of himself as orphan, a pose of essential powerlessness in the social hierarchy, but one of having been abandoned and therefore free from discipline and social responsibility. James wrote of his childhood and memories of reading *David Copperfield*, "Part of the charm of our grandmother's house [in Albany] . . . was its being so much and so sociably a nursuried and playroomed orphanage. . . . Parentally bereft cousins were somehow more thrilling than parentally provided ones" (quoted in Kaplan, 34).[3]

James also cherished another submissive, unmasculine pose—of himself as ill, in need of support because he was physically incapacitated. Oddly, the sickbed assumed aggressive proportions as Henry competed with brother William and sister Alice to see who could most perpetuate illness. Henry had the disadvantage of being essentially robust, so his illnesses when they occurred were valued all the more. In the spring of 1867, Henry boasted of a long list of health concerns, including "mental exhaustion, chronic constipation, stomach problems, eyestrain, and headaches" (Kaplan, 89). Borrowing from his family's wealth of hypochondria, he could feel the distinct advantages of the person in need of nurturing as opposed to one who, in full health, must assume the responsibilities of the world. Again, by submitting to circumstances, in this case illness, one could achieve freedom from responsibility and from the watchful eye of society, who dismissed the sick as momentarily unreliable. Illness begot its own power of sorts.

Sickness also provided James with the excuse to go abroad. Europe was his personal space and had long been associated in American minds with recuperation from the stresses of the New World, the spas of Germany or the ruins of the Mediterranean fostering health for the unhealthy. For James, Europe brought spiritual and intellectual survival for a person stifled by Puritanism. To see himself as physically invalidated by illness would validate his retreat to Europe. If abandoning his family for European climes seemed wrong, illness made it seem right because it was necessary. "His bowels provided him with justification for spending . . . time abroad. The coinage of illness was the most useful currency in the James family" (Kaplan, 111).

Illness also protected him from the social expectation of the all necessary verification of masculinity—the institution of marriage. Illness certainly provided one excuse for James's platonic distance from Minnie Temple. When spiritual reasons for bachelorhood appeared less tenable, James could turn on occasion to the self-construct of illness, in the manner of Ralph Touchett of *The Portrait of a Lady*. Physical infirmity could often find the hard proof of a doctor's diagnosis, whereas James's emotional and spiritual proclivities away from marriage baffled even himself, let alone his family and friends.[4] To see himself at the mercy of nurse and doctor in later years became less a pose than a reality, for his bachelor life left him suicidally lonely and therefore in need of the companionship of a nurturer, even a mother. From sickness on into a near regression back to childhood, James willed himself to be the patient submitting to the kind hand of the benefactor, whether in the form of William James and his wife, Alice Howe Gibbens, or in the form of his close friend Howard Sturgis. To the former, he submitted completely after his breakdown in 1910: he craved "the presence—so beneficent—of my companions" and "caretakers. . . . I utterly cling to them" (quoted in Kaplan, 526). His words to Sturgis make of James the little child: "You are indeed as a missing mother to me, & I, babi-like, (though indeed as if you hadn't Babe enough & to spare!) gurgle back my gratitude" (quoted in Kaplan, 456).

Then again James could play the equally unmasculine role of nursemaid. Far from affecting the masculine role of physician, who prescribes rather than nurtures, James could be the most attentive assistant, providing utterly for the comforts of family members and friends in need. He lavished all good things on visitors from America, such as his sister Alice, visiting Europe to recuperate from bouts of depression, and his Aunt Kate, both of whom took comfort from his complete hospitality on a visit to Liverpool. "Happy to combine the ministrations of both guide and mother substitute," James took over their cares and worries. Aunt Kate wrote to her sister, "[Henry] is always at our door about five or ten minutes before breakfast hour, and if you were to see him invariably folding, in the most precise manner, the shawls and rugs, which are brought in from our drives, and smoothing them down in some quiet corner, with the parasols and umbrellas, tears would flow from your eyes" (quoted in Kaplan, 134).

This self-image of nonaggressiveness need not discount James's simultaneous struggle to coordinate his marginal status with conventions of masculinity that would verify his manhood. Most often his position was mixed; his imaginative portrayals of himself show him walking the thin line between the voice of society and the voice of the self, between conventional male aggression and dangerous unconventionality. His perception of his own ill health perhaps fostered one of his most complex self-images, known famously as his "obscure hurt," which occurred at the time of the Civil War. The dialogue of conflict imposed by the Civil War implied a heightened expectation of society for its males, and to do anything other than serve as a soldier brought into question a man's masculinity. Though James displayed a willingness to serve his time in the military, his father advised against such service.

During this time, James was injured while helping to fight a fire in New York City. By a clever twist of the imagination, he imaginatively linked his personal wound with the public event of the Civil War, seeing in his wound a correspondence with the war's outset. He wrote, "I must have felt in some befooled way in presence of a crisis—the smoke of Charleston Bay still so acrid in the air." He more explicitly drew the connection: "There were hours at which one could scarce have told whether [the wound] came most from one's own poor organism . . . or from the enclosing social body" (quoted in Edel, 1:173). Edel surmises that this intentional confusion "served to minimize [James's] failure during the first six months to enlist with the other young men" (Edel, 1:177). By associating his personal wound with the social body, James imaginatively met the social expectation of manhood. Kaplan explains, "A calibrated injury, one of its effects was to enable him to heighten his consciousness about himself, to create an interesting personal history to substitute for the war experience" (Kaplan, 56). The injury allowed James to be written into history in a personal and fully satisfying manner, with himself as author.

The imagined war wound struggles toward an aggressive impulse in what might otherwise suggest mere passivity. James named this wound his "obscure hurt," perhaps to encourage confusion in his own mind (and in the minds of his readers) about the nature of the wound that had in reality been achieved in relatively banal circumstances. By contrast, a war wound accumulates associations with violence, with romance, with manhood as conceived by social convention.

Paradoxically, the name "obscure hurt" also carries with it associations of sexual incapacity. In naming his wound as "obscure," James concealed it. When he bought the imagined glory of wartime, he paid dearly with the connotation of a wound that must never be advertised. Of all wounds, the only one that is unmentionable is that which would render one sexually incapacitated in a rigorously heterosexual society. Worse yet, one would be thought passive where one had sought to be aggressive, which society might interpret as dangerously androgynous.

However, it remains that James chose the name "obscure hurt" artfully and therefore consciously. Not that every connotation was studied, but his satisfaction with the name suggests a participation in a language far more complex than that offered to the conventional male, for to conceive of oneself as both aggressive and passive meant inevitably to wrestle with the question of an alternative maleness.

But one would be mistaken to think that such a question left James in the lurch, for perhaps only in the middle ground between social expectations of male aggression and the demands of the self could a marginal male find genuine empowerment. For example, James found power in being a master of etiquette, imaginatively conceiving of himself as the arbiter of good taste: "The older I get, the more I hate indelicacy" (quoted in Edel 5:387). Indeed he succeeded in filling that role, best exemplified in the way James was petitioned as a character witness in the romantic affairs of Edith Wharton and Morton Fullerton and Ford Madox Ford and Violet Hunt, who sought him out because of his impeccable character and his kindness.

His taste for decorum placed him once again on the borders between appropriate male aggression and inappropriate passivity. On the one hand, his mastery of manners meant that he could "manhandle" a particular social concept. In addition, James's familiarity with social etiquette allowed him to circumvent in part the need for sexual verification. If he could not prove himself in the sexual realm, he might instead operate capably in the arena of manners, erecting a fortress of good manners that concealed any sexual lack.

On the other hand, James's mastery of manners implies androgyny, a condition of being "in-between" that James found empowering.[5] He squeezed into the androgynous crevices left unguarded by a fiercely heterosexual society by mastering a province that was customarily the domain of women. A man in a woman's world, and yet nonetheless having mastered this realm by dint of being male—James pleasingly united the two in an image of androgynous empowerment. As he would do in other instances, he succeeded in empowering himself in a heterosexual society by writing a fiction for himself that engaged both male and female sensibilities as recognized by society, just enough, follows the argument, to pass in society and yet remain comfortably himself.

James skillfully imagined fictions for himself that end up pleasing society. Much like the gilded surface of his novels and short stories, the fine surface of his life concealed a fierce argument between self and society. The ways James chose to view himself gave him power in a society that would otherwise have threatened such a self with extinction.

Implied in this debate is the relation of the marginal male to women. A central issue for the marginal male is how to accommodate women in his life. While society tells men that they are defined by the women they accompany (and master), the marginal male might well fantasize about life without women. James composed images of himself that time and again address his relations with women and subsequent feelings of masculine unease, repeatedly traversing the fine line between friendship and romance, enjoying the pleasures of a woman's company while avoiding the responsibilities of marriage. The women in his life frequently acted as (one might here employ a term James used in his fiction) "confidantes."[6]

These confidantes affirmed his sense of self in various ways—some dispensed admiration and affection, others simply listened, some entertained him (Sharp, *Confidante*, xiv). In return, these women may have suffered the penalties of the single woman in intimacy with a bachelor. If they anticipated romantic fulfillment, they paid the price of disillusionment. What was said of James's interest in Vernon Lee might be said of his interest in others; that "it had been an egotistical interest and it had not reckoned with the effect it might have on her" (Edel, 3:334-35). "Without any evident sense that women were not for him, he made use of strategies of friendship that readily sacrificed the sexual for the emotionally intimate" (Kaplan, 77). His confidantes included Grace Norton, with whom he corresponded for over forty years; Sarah Butler Wister, who evoked in James a "need to be passive and yet assert himself as a man" (Edel, 149); Isabella Gardner, who shared James's love of fine art; Constance Fenimore Woolson, whose tragic end James saw himself as partly responsible for;[7] Katherine Bronson, a mutual friend of

Woolson and James; Fanny Kemble, a source for *Washington Square*; and not least, Edith Wharton, the beloved companion of his later years.

James's interest in women both answered and denied the voice of society. Convention required that he marry a woman. He never married, but he sought to appease this demand in his own mind by being in the company of women. The admiring female allowed him to answer the call of masculine aggression, inasmuch as he could be the master of the worshipful subject.

In his later years, James's image of himself increasingly accommodated his personal impulses apart from the societal voice demanding that a man be completed with a woman. James turned to young men for consolation who, like the women before them, would help James construct the image of "The Master." Edel calls these young men "acolytes," and suggests that by their faith in James, "his personal *gloire* was assured" (Edel, 3:314). Indeed these men would not have followed James had they not thought him a great man. Had he been anything less in their eyes, men like Hendrik Andersen, Hugh Walpole, and Jocelyn Persse might well have abandoned him. While his friendships with these men likely consisted of more than mere hero worship, still James could profit psychologically from their adoration.

By these various means, James constructed fictions about himself to alleviate his pain in a society bent on restricting a less "qualified" male to the margins. His imagination could protect him from the frightening revelation of too much self. How terrible to suppose that he might have been another Oscar Wilde; how much better to suppose himself above all that. The world of the imagination could save him, he thought. And it did.

Several turn-of-the-century writers, among them Stephen Crane and Theodore Dreiser, were acutely aware of psychological pressures that threatened the individual with annihilation, pressures that were submerged in the unconscious. Included among these writers, James shows characters struggling with forces beyond their control to subdue. In the case of the marginal male, the force is a sexuality that renders him unconventional and thus in danger of psychological destruction. A naked reflection on the self invites catastrophe in a society that has not yet written such behavior into its common parlance, much less begun to regard it as acceptable activity.

However, unlike many writers of the day, who limited their characters to a naturalistic fate, James swerves away from naturalism by empowering his characters with imagination and articulation. Many of James's characters possess superfine sensibilities enhanced by superior education, their already active imaginations feeding on this education, allowing them to articulate (sometimes miraculously) what it is they feel. The oddity is that these same characters who possess superfine sensitivity to others are often slow to achieve awareness of themselves. James's marginal male characters in particular—Lambert Strether, Roderick Hudson, Hyacinth Robinson, the narrator of *The Aspern Papers*, John Marcher—are all abnormally delayed in recognizing their own situations. While some achieve a dazzling recognition late in their careers, others remain permanently blind to aspects of their character crucial to self-understanding, appearing almost unworthy of their superfine sensibilities. Arguably, such characters do not know because they must not know. James investigates the terrain of consciousness to know what a character can bear psychologically. Consciousness is all well and good so long as a character can live with that knowledge, but sometimes consciousness means psychological extinction.

James's marginal males are richly endowed with protective images of themselves. Through a skillful combination of memory and imagination, their pleasing mirror image is "caressingly perpetuated" (Weinstein, *Henry James*, 164). The imagination enables them to confront difficult experience and then speak metaphorically about the experience or about themselves, enough to imaginatively reaffirm their identity.

Like James, these marginal male characters are engaged in a war of fictions between society and the self. Society holds up the conventional image of masculinity (physical aggression, heterosexual activity); meanwhile the marginal male self yearns for atypicality (androgyny, homosexuality, passivity). In earlier James works, the marginal character tends to construct his self-image upon a conventional foundation, imagining himself in an aggressive role that compensates for the relative powerlessness of his situation. This compensation occurs only at a great expense, for while the character achieves wished-for significance in his own mind, he must repress the voice of individuality, characterized in the marginal male by nonaggression.

Later works show James wrestling with this issue in a more complex and satisfying manner, increasingly allowing the marginal male to shed the aggression of conventional masculinity in favor of a heightened androgyny, implying increased risk. Exactly how much can a character answer the needs of the self and still survive as a social being? In these later fictions, the tension is greater as James's marginal male characters struggle to find the balance in a dialogue between self and society.

Rowland Mallet of *Roderick Hudson* provides an early example of a marginal character possessing the psychic protection of a vivid imagination. While many readers find Rowland an engaging study in the process of "heightened awareness," in some ways he is the most blind of all James's marginal males. Were he to acknowledge the truth of his situation he might risk psychological destruction, bereft as he is of the social moorings of marriage and family. Like James's other marginal males, Rowland must invent a position for himself in society by the ways he thinks and talks about himself.

As one discovers in James's life, the marginal male of vivid imagination can imagine himself either as society would wish to see a man, or as the self instructs. Were such a male to compose a fiction from inner voices, the image would be one of androgyny. However, Rowland Mallet imagines himself in aggressive roles that conform to the demands of society (though in reality his character is nonaggressive).

Mallet's meager reality is one of subservience to Roderick, Mrs. Hudson, and Mary Garland. He expends considerable energy to achieve significance, while in fact he is consigned to the margins. People use Rowland briefly, never permitting him lasting significance in their lives. To compensate for this marginalization, Rowland has flights of fancy, imagining himself as he thinks a man should be—significant and powerful. In his imagination, he likes to think of himself as a father of sorts to Roderick, having been charged by Mrs. Hudson to raise him in her absence. He says with self-importance, "I have undertaken to answer to . . . his mother for his doing well" (*Roderick Hudson*, 229). The narrator calls this need to be fatherly Rowland's "paternal conscience" (65).

The comfort this image affords cannot be overstated, for it places Rowland in a role that society would deny him. Bachelor that he is, he will probably never parent a child. Denied the social benediction of fatherhood, he writes his own script, imagining himself to be significantly older (though Rowland himself is introduced to the reader as a "young man"), and more experienced (although he is not insofar as he customarily resists spontaneity and change). Still, Rowland will believe, as he says to Roderick, that "I am older than you and know the world better" (78). He repeatedly fictionalizes the father-son relationship by speaking to Roderick in condescending tone and diction, addressing Roderick on one occasion as "My dear boy" (139) and in moments of a father's righteous indignation crying out, "Oh, miserable boy!" (224).

His sense of being a father spawns an elaborate plan of leading the "younger" Roderick to a full display of his artistic talent. Like a wise father, Rowland will gently persuade rather than force: his "theory of his own duty" is to let Roderick run his course and play his cards, prepared to point out shoals and pitfalls and administer "a friendly propulsion through tight places" (113).

Rowland's sense of paternalism is backed by Victorian earnestness. The narrator refers to his "familiar chronic sense of his duties," his "excellent cause" (380), and his "desire to serve" (356). With draconian rigidity he will not joke about a serious matter like Roderick's artistic potential. While Roderick would "laugh extravagantly," Rowland "sat perfectly grave, on principle" (138), imbued with a sense of missionary zeal and a father's sense of destiny for his "son." When Roderick fails to meet Rowland's expectations, the father grieves over the prodigal: "He had tried to be wise, he had tried to be kind, he had engaged in an estimable enterprise; but his wisdom, his kindness, his energy, had been thrown back in his face" (248). The narrator mocks Rowland's image of himself by punning on the word *pity* as Rowland tours the Pitti Palace (250).

The concept of the father suggests Rowland's tendency to conform to the ideal of adult masculinity. The father retains patriarchal authority by virtue of superior experience and wisdom, precisely as Rowland claims. The father is an aggressive figure seeking to force his views on his "son," however gently this force may appear. In Rowland's consciousness of filling an aggressive role, he fails to hear his own inner impulses. The reader leaves this novel disliking Rowland because he remains blind to his own voice—what is it exactly that he wants? James's early exploration of the self-imaging of a marginal figure shows a man grasping for an image of masculinity which turns back upon itself as it sows the seeds of contradiction and ultimate failure.

Because the fiction he has written as father is ill-suited for him, Rowland is doomed to failure. He fails by attempting to fulfill another competing role, that of lover. While attempting to be the wise patriarch to Roderick, he divides his energy by playing the secret lover of Mary Garland, who functions in the novel as the reward for the man who most scrupulously adheres to social convention as written by American culture. She insists on her dislike of European decadence, favoring the innocence of America. The man who will succeed with her must win her approval both romantically and intellectually. Of course, Rowland is doomed from the outset because Mary doesn't care about him at all, but also, and more profoundly, because of his conflicting efforts to be both father and lover.

Rowland's desire for Mary opposes his imagined goal of Roderick's success, for if Roderick succeeds as Rowland the Father intends, then Roderick will wed Mary. Rowland views her as a reward for Roderick if he maintains some respectability, asking himself, "What right had a man who was engaged to that delightful girl in Northampton to behave as if his consciousness were a common blank, to be overlaid with coarse sensations?" (136). Rowland here plays the role of the father expressing righteous indignation about his son's failure to achieve respectability and wed a proper young woman.

On the other hand, if Roderick fails in terms of respectability, Roderick will lose Mary, and Rowland could, he imagines, win her for himself. Because of this, Rowland paradoxically yearns for the "son's" failure at the same time that he encourages his success. When Roderick falls so low in respectability that he can beg Mary for money, Rowland "felt a movement of irrepressible elation, and he barely stifled a cry of joy. Now, surely, Roderick had shattered the last link in the chain that bound Mary to him, and after this she would be free!" (373). The voice speaking here is the voice of the Rowland the Lover in hot pursuit of the beloved.

Surprisingly, in the contradictory stance fostered by denial, Rowland comes out victorious in terms of his psyche, insofar as the real battle of the marginal male is with the voice that proclaims the insignificance of the self. That voice is an inner one, and it is deadly. Rowland's blindness to his precarious masculinity actually protects him from self-annihilation. However, the cost is that he is hollow and therefore unlikable as a fictional character. Inwardly he succeeds, at the expense of outer failure. The success of Rowland's blindness is exemplified in his final struggle with Roderick. In this scene, Roderick has rightly condemned Rowland for being out of touch with his passion and refusing to admit it. Rowland practices denial with astonishing proficiency: "Roderick's words seemed at first to Rowland like something heard in a dream; it was impossible they had been actually spoken" (374). In a venomous tone, Rowland says to Roderick, "We will let this pass," implying that they should both forget Roderick's words. While Roderick has all along seemed the more powerful of the two, the supposedly weaker Rowland here "manhandles" the conversation, leaving Roderick suicidal while fortifying his own sense of rightness. Through denial of the self, Rowland remains immune to destructive tendencies, at the novel's end behaving much as the reader found him at the beginning—remotely attracted to Mary Garland. The novel ends with Rowland safely ensconced in his image of the betrayed father.

While Rowland Mallet succeeds through denial of the self, composing fictions that conform to the aggressive masculine images of "father" and "lover," another marginal male in James's work finds only annihilation. Some ten years after the publication of *Roderick Hudson*, James returned to a thoroughgoing study of the marginal male, this time in the form of an entirely nonaggressive young man. As was mentioned in chapter one of this study, Hyacinth Robinson of *The Princess Casamassima* epitomizes the male of unconventional masculinity: he is "small," he has a "narrow chest" and a "pale complexion," his figure is "childishly slight," and his hands are "delicate" (*Princess Casamassima*, 104). More significant than his meager physicality is his ambivalence regarding men, women, sexuality, and power. "He would never marry at all—to that his mind was absolutely made up; he would never hand on to another the burden which had made his own young spirit so intolerably sore, the inheritance which had darkened the whole threshold of his manhood." Particularly in his dealings with women, he is aware of his unconventionality: "The society of women was to be enjoyed on other terms" (105), meaning friendship rather than marriage.

Whereas in *Roderick Hudson* James portrays a character equipped with the imaginative tools necessary to moor himself psychologically, here James asks the question, What if an unconventional character lacks a vivid imagination? While Rowland Mallet succeeds in convincing himself of the truth of the fictions he has created, Hyacinth remains unconvinced of any sense of self.

One element that prevents Hyacinth from possessing psychological security is his vague recollection of inner longings. Whereas Rowland Mallet abandons the inner self altogether for the roles society assigns him, Hyacinth is haunted by weak echoes of his own voice. Hyacinth "wished to go through life in his own character; but he checked himself, with the reflection that this was exactly what, apparently, he was destined not to do." With customary ambivalence, he is aware vaguely of his own impulses, and yet checks them when he hears the appeal of the more powerful voices of society. "His own character? He was to cover that up as carefully as possible; he was to go through life in a mask, in a borrowed mantle; he was to be, every day and every hour, an actor" (109). Hearing the dialogue between self and society, he cannot commit himself to either.

To add to his confusion, the voices of society are themselves contradictory. "He had in a word, more impressions than he knew what to do with—felt sometimes as if they would consume or asphyxiate him" (158). One voice is that of the highly aggressive revolutionary Paul Muniment, who seeks to force his world vision on society. That Hyacinth listens to him implies a need to act upon the world as Muniment has done, with force.

On the other hand, Christina (the Princess Casamassima) speaks for nonaggression, encouraging nonviolence and an appreciation of the arts. By implication, all that she is associated with becomes feminized. Hyacinth's attraction to the "flower of high civilization" (165) as displayed by the Princess suggests that his alignment with the feminized world is equally as strong as his sympathy for Muniment's conventionally masculine realm. Her world is associated with the passive, Muniment's with the active. As Madame Grandoni says in reference to the now hectic pace of Hyacinth's life under Paul Muniment, "For an active young man like [Hyacinth] Robinson, going every day to his work, there is nothing more exhausting than such an unoccupied life as ours. For what do we do, after all?" (319-20). Their lives are composed of the passive and the luxurious.

James intends Hyacinth's precarious position to be between the masculine and feminine. Like Rowland, Hyacinth starts out from a precarious position as a marginal male. Unlike Rowland, he is led further down the path of ambiguity. Whereas Rowland concretizes images of himself, Hyacinth remains unsure of his identity, adrift between impulses from within and admonitions from without. "There were times when he said to himself that it might very well be his fate to be divided, to the point of torture, to be split open by sympathies that pulled him in different ways" (165). In the metaphors employed by Hyacinth, one senses already the deadliness of being so divided. In the end, having failed to affirm the "truth" of any one fiction of the self, Hyacinth commits suicide. James employs the term "vague" to describe Hyacinth's final condition before his death (582).

Later in the same decade in which he wrote *The Princess Casamassima*, James continued his exploration of the marginal male in *The Aspern Papers*. The narrator of *The Aspern Papers* offers yet another study in protective images of the self, though he is less savory, even wicked, when compared with characters heretofore mentioned. In this case, the marginal male again is torn between conventional masculinity and personal inclination. The voice of society encourages him to participate in the fictions of legendary romance: he is at once adventurer, hunter, and romancer—the man on a quest. On the other hand he demonstrates a profound remoteness from heterosexuality. While he will lie, steal, perhaps even murder to obtain the Aspern papers, he will not follow Aspern's lead into the world of heterosexuality: "He fears marriage more than he loves Aspern" (Kaplan 319).

The narrator of *The Aspern Papers* participates in a meager reality in terms of conventional manhood. His most disconcerting moment occurs just after Miss Tita has proposed marriage to him. He rejects her (symptomatic of his marginality), and now tours the city on foot or by gondola, seeking consolation from the shock of Miss Tita's proposal. "I don't know why it happened that on this occasion I was more than ever struck with that queer air of sociability, of cousinship and family life, which makes up half the expression of Venice" (*Aspern Papers*, 248). He sees Venice as a stage on which everyone but himself is a player. His lack of an acceptable role invites fantasies of conventional manhood. As a scholar in pursuit of the Aspern papers, he frames his occupation in an exclusively male fashion to the point of violence, which he happily associates with masculinity.

His masculine image is not that of the father, as in the case of Rowland, but of the scholar turned conqueror. He couches his academic life in the rhetoric of heroism: "My eccentric private errand became a part of the general romance and the general glory" (181). Speaking of himself and a fellow scholar, he says, "We held, justly, as I think, that we had done more for [Aspern's] memory than anyone else, and we had done it by opening lights into his life" (155-56). The narrator's rhetoric allows him to embellish his academic task to the point of beatific radiance: "I felt even a mystic companionship, a moral fraternity with all those who in the past had been in the service of art. They had worked for beauty, for a devotion; and what else was I doing?" (181). He associates his task with brotherhood; his is a masculine duty demanding the highest devotion and rigor, a type of aggression that he feels no woman could carry out.

Consequently, the narrator feels licensed to abuse women. In his world, violence toward the female promotes one's occupational ends. He imagines that Juliana's death will help him gain access to the Aspern papers. "She would die next week, she would die tomorrow—then I could seize her papers" (168). It would even be acceptable if he initiates the violent act. When he confronts Juliana's death, his way of minimizing his guilt is nothing short of outrageous—and hilarious:

> It had been devilish awkward, as the young men say, to be found by Juliana in the dead of night examining the attachment of her bureau; and it had not been less so to have to believe for a good many hours afterward that it was highly probable I had killed her. In writing to Miss Tita I attempted to minimize these irregularities. (234)

Juliana alive and well is a barrier to his ends; her elimination provides him access, so he thinks, to his exclusively masculine goal.

The narrator commits verbal violence on women. His catalog of pejoratives for Juliana is lengthy: she is "a sarcastic, profane, cynical old woman" (202) and a "cynical old witch" (216). She is a "bad economist" as well; the narrator has never heard of "such a waste of material" (166). His thoughts of Miss Tita are equally violent in terms of character assassination. His seemingly objective criticism carries the taint of mockery when he describes Miss Tita as having large eyes that however are "not bright," and a great deal of hair that, however, is "not 'dressed,' " and "long fine hands which were—possibly—not clean" (163). He judges her intellect as "small" and "unsophisticated" (237).

The violence is carried out in other ways as well, complicating the narrator's relationship with women. At the same time that he finds women utterly despicable because they impede his male-oriented goal, he also finds them necessary. For example, he could commit psychological violence on the housekeeper, Olimpia, and so twist her to his purposes. He thinks of how he might "corrupt" her; or rephrased in more forceful terms, how the "faithful domestic" might perhaps "be managed" (209). He commits romantic/sexual violence on the useful Miss Tita by courting her with verbal and physical cues in order to manipulate her to his scholar's purposes, then abandoning her. The narrator dismisses Miss Tita, first by degrees in moments of scathing criticism, and then outright when he decides that marriage is worse than any other baseness he might commit: "I could not, for a bundle of tattered papers, marry a ridiculous, pathetic, provincial old woman" (247). At his weakest moment, when he admits to having "deplorably trifled," it is the horror of marriage that saves him. Self-protectively, he decides that he "hadn't given her cause" to wish to marry him.

This romantic treachery allows the narrator to be physically in nearly continuous company with women, in what he conceives of as a highly conventional male role (the scholar-conqueror), and yet remain sexually detached, as if the heterosexual component did not exist. Never before in his fiction had James so thoroughly tested the limits of the marginal male's capacity for denial. To what extent can a marginal male write himself into a fictional world while surrounding himself with the very heterosexuality that threatens to dissolve him? Rowland Mallet in *Roderick Hudson* saw Mary Garland in romantic terms, but remained safely remote, physically and geographically. In contrast, the *Aspern* narrator lives in relative intimacy with women. He can do so because he adopts a defensive posture. Women are recognized for what they are to him—a threat. He does whatever is necessary to maintain his distance, perceiving them as temporarily useful but ultimately evil and committing all manner of violence upon them to reach his goal.

This character is successful but terrifying. James has constructed a character endlessly secure in the fictive role in which he imagines himself—the scholar-conqueror—working toward virtuous and asexual ends. However, the man is a monster. Having imagined a fiction that is conventionally masculine in its obsession for all things male—aggression, the hunt, violence—this character denies the sexual interpretation of his actions, perhaps the root cause of his rabid posture toward women's sexuality. His posturing of aggression is narrow and constricting, masking the necessary sexual component that makes a person complete. In the end the reader is left with a fascinating machine-more-than-human. Having risked nothing, he remains buried in a fiction of self-denial.

What looms large for James and his marginal male is how such a man can appropriately relate to women. It would seem up to this point that a mutually satisfying relationship between women and the marginal male is not possible. Not until *The Ambassadors* would James find some resolution to that question. Lambert Strether more than any other marginal figure sacrifices the voices of conventional masculinity to the interest of voices from within, including that of his sexuality. The fictions he composes for himself represent the awakening of personal desires and simultaneously represent a more satisfying (though unconventional) relationship with women. It would seem that the more conventional masculinity is sacrificed, the more a marginal male can see his way to letting women into his life. Still the picture is far from perfect.

In *The Ambassadors*, James portrays a marginal male of considerable introspection when compared with either Rowland Mallet or the narrator of *The Aspern Papers*. Lambert Strether has the ability to look inward and see the frightening image of himself. Most often, his inward journey brings him to the truth of his empty past. He has married, he has a child, but his capacity for passion has gone untried. His experience in Paris is a prolonged recognition of the need for passion and the attempt to express it, however belatedly. His imagines Paris as a glittering jewel with facets too numerous for easy comprehension. The only way to get at Paris at all is to live there for some time, to come to terms with the "immediate and the sensible" that Paris has to offer. In Paris, Strether smokes his first cigarette. He attends lavish parties and visits theaters and museums. He says, "I don't get drunk; I don't pursue the ladies; I don't spend money; I don't even write sonnets. But nevertheless I'm making up late for what I didn't have early" (*Ambassadors*, 197).

And in Paris he comes closer than ever before to the truth of sexual intimacy, acknowledging there the terror of real intimacy as expressed by Madame de Vionnet and Chad. More terrifying still, he must confront the embarrassment of his not having known more about sexual intimacy at an earlier stage in life. Maturity has become a psychological liability for Strether since he must confront at every step of the way what he should have known before.

In Strether's case, the question is how he manages psychologically to cope with such self-discovery. While Rowland Mallet and *Aspern's* narrator remain blind to the bitter end, Strether's forays bring him dangerously close to a crisis of identity. Strether imagines himself as "touching bottom" (316), feeling that he has been "living almost disgracefully from hand to mouth." Then again he makes a "private concession to cowardice" (171), or he feels "silly" (212), or wonders "if he felt as the impudent feel" (271). Finally he wonders if "he didn't *look* demoralised and disreputable" though he "hadn't yet struck himself, since leaving Woollett, so much as a loafer" (316). More than other marginal male characters, Strether is able to accept potentially disruptive images of himself, demonstrating a quality of surrender that places him at risk.

Perhaps his greatest risk comes in his emotional nakedness at the end of the novel. Strether resolves to return to America because he recognizes that he has no future in Paris. The friends whom he trusted find him marginally useful but not central to their lives. However, the America he will return to is equally empty of friends, as he does not return to the same America that he left behind. Bereft of the psychic comforts afforded a conventional male in the conventions of family and marriage, Strether appears suicidally vulnerable.

What then are Strether's psychological "security blankets"? Rowland Mallet and the narrator of The Aspern Papers conjured images of conventional masculinity. One was a father figure, carrying the thoroughly masculine weight of the patriarchy; the other was the scholar-hunter seeking the male-oriented goal of another man's writing—a world created by men and for men.

Strether likewise composes fictions, but his fictions present a masculinity of a different order, constructed around surrender and accommodation. Whereas the earlier images were aggressive, Strether's constructions are passive. The quality of surrender operates both in the form that his images take and in the effect of those images. The result is that Strether varies from the normative image of the aggressive male, and he pays the price of not appearing fearsome to his peers. He is useful to those around him because he is pliable, and of course likable—primed for exploitation. Despite the risk, Strether ends up miraculously intact. The question James tries to answer with Strether is, How much can a marginal figure write fictions from his inner impulses and still survive in a conventional world? Lyall H. Powers has noted this effort of James to "examine the problem of learning to live in a 'civilized' society whose manners, conventions, prejudices often threaten individual integrity; of coming to terms with that society's demands; and of managing to make the necessary compromises—but without giving up one's essential self" (as quoted in Weatherby, James Baldwin, 85). Strether composes an alternative masculinity of surrender as opposed to aggression, risking his survival in a heterosexual society.

This unique quality of surrender governs the way Strether sees his entire life to this point. Nostalgia renders him passive—the past is simply the past and nothing can be done about it. He finds relief at the sorrowful yet strangely pleasurable moments when he can surrender to the sense of having missed out on some irrecoverable joy. The novel is filled with instances, as with little Bilham, when Strether releases tension by denying the possibility of changing his situation. The past is a "great gray desert" in Strether's mind, and that is how it will always remain: "Everything represented the substance of his loss" (281). While it might appear strange that there should be pleasure in precisely what he warns little Bilham against, nonetheless the reader watches Strether revel "luxuriously" in the sense of his meager past (61). Such an act brings the bliss of passivity rather than the strain of active participation.

Strether's alternative to male aggressiveness is also demonstrated in the images he chooses for himself. While other male characters strain after conventional images of male domination, Strether contents himself with the image of a little boy. One of numerous examples comes when Strether chastises himself for not finding more time to speak with Chad at their first meeting in the theater. He imagines himself a child: "He had stuck there like a schoolboy wishing not to miss a minute of the show" (91).[8]

The image of the boy oddly enough empowers Strether, for he can now look at his life with the wide margin of forgiveness allowed a mischievous child. If he is the little boy, then other adults must shoulder the burdens of parents or disciplinarians, nurturing him in his time of need, or punishing him if he has been "bad." Other people symbolically carry responsibility, where he as the child is relieved of guilt or the burden of decision-making. His is a temporary flight into irresponsibility; accordingly, Maria Gostrey assumes the role of mother to her "boy." Strether's fantasy of childhood unites with his fantasy of being "bad." He imagines himself as the child sitting at the feet of the motherly Maria Gostrey: "He sat at her feet and held on by her garment and was fed by her hand" (196). And if Maria is the mother, then he is the toddler: "He could toddle alone. . . . The time seemed already far off when he had held out his small thirsty cup to the spout of her pail" (195). If he has done wrong, now it becomes a childish wrong, with Mrs. Newsome or one of her representatives as disciplinarian. "He saw himself, under [Sarah Pocock's] direction, recommitted to Woollett as juvenile offenders are committed to reformatories" (201). Strether's extended metaphor of childish offense and punishment is tangled with associations that place him as the victim of excessive punishment at the hands of oppressive authorities.

Part of the sense of childhood comes in his figuring his sojourn in Europe as an "escape" and an "adventure." This vocabulary celebrates the childish thrill in the unknown, an exuberance that would be subdued in a figure who perceived himself as adult. Every moment away from Woollett or the figures who symbolize Woollett is itself an adventure. He "escapes" from Waymarsh (34) just as he "runs away" from Mrs. Newsome (33). The difference between Woollett and Europe is no less than the difference between the banality of adulthood and the exuberance of childhood—"He was there on some chance of feeling the brush of the wing of the stray spirit of youth. He felt it in fact, he had it beside him" (67). His association of Europe with youth is clear when says to Maria, "Of course I'm youth—youth for the trip to Europe. I began to be young, or at least to get the benefit of it, the moment I met you at Chester" (197). On another occasion, in a "great dim church," he images himself as a young man, a "student" appreciating the charm of the edifice (171).

At one moment he imagines himself the innocent child, but at the next he can be an old man too far gone in years to repair his failures with fresh successes. "Strether relapsed into the sense—which had for him in these days most of comfort—that he was free to believe in anything that from hour to hour kept him going" (262). He changes as his mind changes to cope with terrors of experience. The image of the old man, like that of the little boy, is paradoxically passive in its maleness, figuring prominently in Strether's imagination at moments when he looks back over the long road of life and finds his life wanting in so many ways. One example comes in his discussion with little Bilham on living life to the fullest, when he says, "I haven't done so enough before—and now I'm old; too old at any rate for what I see" (132). The statement is inaccurate when applied to his years, for the narrator describes Strether as middle-aged. Strether appears to will an alternative masculinity by the fictions he composes for himself. Whether in old age or pre-adolescence, he finds psychological comfort in images that answer more to his own impulses toward androgyny than to those of society.

Strether also composes an androgynous image. He is the healer, a role stereotypically associated with women; the healer comes to the aid of those in need of nurturing. Strether fills this role in relation to Waymarsh, who represents the male patient in need of the gentle/feminine touch. Strether's role as nurse is best seen when he assists Waymarsh in bedding down for the night, turning down the lamp and making sure his companion has plenty of blankets. After this odd moment of self-sacrifice to the self-pitying Waymarsh, Strether imagines his companion as "a patient in a hospital" (33). Strether's unusual role continues the following morning when he plays maid to Waymarsh's demands for breakfast. His companion has "laid upon" Strether "dreadful divined responsibilities in respect to beefsteak and oranges" (35). He sees himself as endlessly useful: "I sort of feel . . . that the whole thing will come upon me. Yes, I shall have every inch and every ounce of it. I shall be *used* for it—! . . . To the last drop of my blood" (244). He becomes a beast of burden: "I've come very much, it seems to me, to double up my fore legs in the manner of the camel when he gets down on his knees to make his back convenient" (284). Not only does Strether accept his alternative masculinity; he cultivates it in the fictions he creates for himself.

However, the picture is complicated by Strether's emotional intimacy with a woman. As with earlier marginal figures, Strether's interaction with women acts as a barometer of self-awareness. A healthy interaction with women demands that the marginal male unburden himself of the baggage of false images that promote a deep-seated aggression toward women. A marginal male who operates only within conventional fictions finds only frustration, which might lead him to harm himself or others.

Strether's relation with women is more self-satisfying than that of James's earlier marginal males. Whereas Rowland Mallet is theoretically committed to romance, in reality he is thoroughly platonic. Hyacinth Robinson is gentle but confused; his relationship with the Princess Casamassima lacks eroticism. The erotic tension between the narrator of *The Aspern Papers* and Miss Tita is essentially violent. However, with Lambert Strether, James opens the door to a healthier relationship between the marginal male and the female confidante.

Strether surrenders to Maria Gostrey at the risk of committing himself to more intimacy than he is prepared for. Prior to his meeting her, he has denied women knowledge of his private affairs, fencing women out by denying their ability to think and reason to the degree that men can. Maria is apparently one of the few women in whom he acknowledges intellectual validity: "He had quite the sense that she knew things he didn't, and though this was a concession that in general he found not easy to make to women, he made it now as good-humouredly as if it lifted a burden" (22). Strether surrenders to her equality, even her superiority, with regard to his affairs. He establishes an intimacy with Maria that places himself at risk: if he invests too much in their relationship, he might commit himself to more than he has bargained for.

To protect himself, Strether must constantly redefine the relationship to his satisfaction. His dialogue with the feminine entails his ignoring the heterosexual script. The contrivance of such a nonheterosexual text means that immediate attention must be given to the role that a woman plays in his life. If he is to allow Maria access to his life, he must strictly define her role to prevent her from assuming more power in his fiction than he intends. For example, he can safely view her as a "woman of fashion" who expertly guides him into European high society (38). He can also define their relationship by comparing Maria to nonsexual partners of his past—Waymarsh and Mrs. Newsome (61). Maria helps him establish a sense of safety by imaging them as "beaten brothers in arms" (40).

Within established boundaries, Maria has much to offer the marginal Strether. After their meeting, Strether is free to explore his own psyche and then retreat to the denlike security and warmth of Maria's conversation to alleviate his pain. Ready enough restore his ego, she begins by telling him how much she loves his name (23), verbally creating in him a sense of trust, even saying to him outright, "You trust me" (25). As Sister M. Corona Sharp observes, "The sympathy and kindness of [Maria], as well as her own confidence inspire [Strether] with trust" (Sharp, 153). She listens always with interest, what James terms on one occasion "charming earnestness" (27), and by comparing Strether to others, she helps him imagine his superiority. Comparing Strether to Mrs. Newsome, Maria says he is "the bigger swell of the two" (51). At other times abstractions suffice: "You're always wonderful!" (191). Maria becomes so much for him that Strether imagines he cannot function without her. "She was the blessing that had now become his need, and what could prove it better than that without her he had lost himself?" (80).

Strether views Maria as a utility. "It was all he needed that she liked him enough for what they were doing" (326). From his perspective, the success of their relationship depends on how little Maria and he talk about themselves, because such talk would complicate their relationship. "The essential freshness of a relation so simple was a cool bath to the soreness produced by other relations" (326). What Strether wants is a relationship with Maria that clarifies other relationships. Maria is to be the sounding board upon which Strether can deflect problems in his more "serious" relations. If for a moment their friendship was to become the center of his life, it would threaten to throw everything else off balance.

The positive element of this relationship—something new in the marginal male's relations with women—is that the woman also gains something. Strether is most curious to know why Maria wants to help him. She first assures him that it is not for money. In fact, she says, "I don't do it for any particular advantage" (26). Still, the course of their friendship reveals definite satisfaction: Maria enjoys vicariously the thrill of Strether's European adventures: "Miss Gostrey drank it in" (240). With near voyeuristic pleasure, she feeds on every detail he cares to share with her. She loves nothing more than to go out on the town and then to return alone to meditate on what she has seen and heard. Such has been her habit "of wet nights after pleasures, thinking things over, on the return, in lonely four-wheelers" (52). She thrills in seeing Strether work things out on his own. "To see you work it out would will be one of the sensations of my life" (192).

However, Strether's resistance to the dialogue of heterosexual romance becomes increasingly difficult. Because Maria and he live inescapably in a heterosexual world, their words are drawn into a fiction of romance between man and woman. Much of what they say carries the weight of double entendre. When Strether says to Maria, "Oh but I feel to-day that I shall want you yet," he may intend an expression of friendship, but his words carry the symbolic weight of romance. While Strether resists this meaning, Maria appears to accept these conventions, imagining that he wishes to be her lover. When he says, "I want you here" (292), she can imagine that Strether means what he may not. Maria's words, on the other hand, can absolve her of initiating any threat to Strether's independence, all the while affirming romance. She says, "There's a service—possible for you to render—that I know, all the same, I shall think of" (198). Though she never mentions the words "romance" or "marriage," still the dialogue in which they find themselves embroiled renders the text romantic. Finally, time is on the side of convention. The longer the lives of Maria and Strether intertwine, the less Strether can resist the fiction that has already been written for Maria and himself.

Society acts as a mirror for Strether's deepest fears. Madame de Vionnet seems unable to resist the chance to view Maria and Strether as romantically attached when she declares how pleased she is at Maria's new-found "happiness."

Whether she intends this meaning or not, Strether jumps to that conclusion. "What it conveyed was that *he* was Maria Gostrey's happiness." He "challenges the thought"; it is so abhorrent to him that he recoils with a "smothered inward shudder" (162). Later Madame de Vionnet makes her assumptions more explicit when she begins to pair up men with women. Being so enmeshed in the fiction of heterosexual romance herself, she cannot resist the easy pairing of Maria with Strether: "You've got Maria" (233). Strether responds reluctantly, "And Maria had got me. So it goes." His last words sound the note of helplessness. He appears to recognize the script that has been written for him, which if taken to its conclusion, inevitably pairs him with the nearest woman, in this case Maria Gostrey.

And here commences the ugliness of the relationship. James shows a friendship between a marginal male and a female confidante at the limits of its success. The two texts inevitably clash; each does violence to the integrity of the other. Strether threatens Maria with his irreducible individuality that denies her romantic inclinations. Maria threatens Strether by her participation in conventional romance. True, theirs is not the intended brutality acted out by the narrator of *The Aspern Papers*. Still it is violence of a sort, for it necessitates the refusal of one text in favor of another. Despite all of Strether's gentleness in comparison with other male characters heretofore examined, his will to power entails an ultimate rejection of the outer fiction in favor of a fiction of his own creation.

In the last scene of the novel, Maria's words are so caught up in the rhetoric of heterosexual romance that she appears to intend a betrayal of her feelings for Strether. She says, "There's nothing, you know, I wouldn't do for you." And then as if to clinch her romantic intention she adds, "There's nothing in all the world" (344). Lest their be any doubt as to the implications of Maria Gostrey's invitation, Mary Doyle Springer elucidates the potentially sinister connection between Maria's "traditional caretaking role" and the "official law" of society as defined by Julia Kristeva (Springer, "Closure," 278). Strether cannot remain nonaggressive if aggressivity means defending oneself against the complexities of a patriarchal society that even the perpetrator, in this case Maria, may not herself be aware of, so appealingly "normal" is her desire to be with Strether in his later years.

Springer defines Strether's nervous stammering in the final passages of the novel as his desperate attempts to elude Maria's conventional romantic discourse (Springer, 278). Strether's response places them at odds with each other in competing fictions that can never be resolved to the satisfaction of both parties. His near resolution (and so it is James's as well) is "Then there we are." These words situate them in time and place, but a time and place of Strether's choosing. He "wins" if winning means choosing freely. He finds himself free while Maria finds herself alone.

Strether finally stands in a position of power within his own fiction. The impulses of marginality have asked that he surrender the aggression conventionally associated with the male ego. In return he has allowed for an accommodation of emotional intimacy with a woman to a degree unmatched by James's earlier marginal male figures. Strether surrenders to the point where society asks of him what he cannot bear, and from that low vantage point he must return to a position of ultimate defensiveness. The marginal male cannot survive without an ultimate aggressive stance against the tyranny of conventional society. James implies in this novel the positive aspects to be gained from a fiction that accommodates inner impulses, but he also implies coming to terms with an inherent lack of resolution between conventional society and the individual.

"The Beast in the Jungle" offers perhaps the definitive statement of James on the marginal male and sexuality. James has placed John Marcher at psychological risk in order to test fully the powers of the imagination in operation against sexual awareness, and the author appears to side finally with deception over potential psychological disaster. Sexuality has all along been the central issue and the greatest challenge for the marginal male; it is the basis for his marginality. While *The Ambassadors* asks how much the individual can answer to inner impulses and still survive in a fiercely heterosexual world, "The Beast in the Jungle" returns to the safety of delusion and adds that such delusion is not only likely but *necessary* in the time and place James wrote about.

Marcher imagines himself in the aggressive role of the hunter, a conventional male role; he is on a hunt after some wild beast that will spring at some unknown point in the future and change his life forever. James wants his marginal male abundantly equipped to deal with the threat to his psyche. Marcher must maximize the conventional maleness in what is really a highly unconventional situation; seeing himself as a hunter might somehow compensate for his bachelor status.

Marcher aligns himself with convention by placing himself in the company of a woman. Like Strether, Marcher enjoys the benefits of a confidante. May Bartram reinforces Marcher's image of himself. Her perspective curiously lacks the irony, even sarcasm, that Marcher has grown accustomed to in past relationships. "If she didn't take the sarcastic view she clearly took the sympathetic, and that was what he had, in all the long time, from no one whomsoever" ("Beast in the Jungle," 335). As his "kind wise keeper" (344), May affirms his positive self-image by concealing him from the object of his hunt. While he has figured the great event as horrible indeed, the imagined beast lacks the horror of the *thing* itself, whatever *it* is. It is the real beast that May conceals from Marcher. In opposition to the customary aims of the confidante, May adopts the mission of concealment rather than illumination. She aims finally to keep Marcher from suffering. She believes first of all that what they have considered between them as the possible beast is not the beast after all. She has named a "great many" possibilities to Marcher, but the reader is to assume that what she feels has *not* been named. It is the thing "I've never said," she tells him. With superior knowledge (she has been assigned attributes of a sybil and a sphinx) she tells him that, thanks to her secrecy, Marcher will "never" consciously suffer.

The expense to May is great indeed. It is clear that society excuses a bachelor for the company he keeps with a woman. It not only excuses him, but tacitly praises him for being "man enough" to attract a woman. And if sex is involved, all the better. Marcher admits, "You help me to pass for a man like another" (353). On the other hand, May pays a considerable price because her unmarried status lacks the sanction of bachelorhood. A woman must marry to accompany a man without censure: every walk in public with John Marcher compromises May's respectability. May says, "I never said that it hadn't made me a good deal talked about." And later: "I don't pretend it exactly shows that I'm not living for you. It's my intimacy with you that's in question" (353).

This conflict makes May his greatest enemy. True, she is the friend of his ego in the sense that she affirms his imagined view of himself. She is his enemy, however, in her romantic sentiments for him. May approaches Marcher with a feminine sexuality he finally cannot deny: "It had become suddenly, from her movement and attitude, beautiful and vivid to him that she had something more to give him; her wasted face delicately shone with it—it glittered almost as with the white lustre of silver in her expression" (365). More obviously in another instance, she "showed herself, all draped and all soft, in her fairness and slimness" (363).

Perhaps no greater proof of her romance, and therefore of their antagonism, exists than in the psychological defenses Marcher constructs against her. His imagination spins elaborate pictures to shut May out. Indeed the central image of his life, the hunt for the beast in the jungle, is noticeably bereft of women. "A man of feeling didn't cause himself to be accompanied by a lady on a tiger hunt. Such was the image under which he had ended by figuring his life" (343). Only after May dies can Marcher safely view her love for him in its fullness. Only when she presents no living threat to his psyche can his imagination allow her love to penetrate his consciousness.

Here resides perhaps the strongest evidence of the marginal male's need for a protective imagination. James never more eloquently expresses the need for the imagination in securing oneself against psychological destruction than in the case of John Marcher. Marcher's skillful imagination keeps him from imagining still deeper secrets about himself. The secret of May's love for him, and his defense against it, are but secondary to the major threat, a threat from within: his own sexuality. He responds rather simplistically after her death with the answer, "The escape would have been to love her; then, *then* he would have lived." However, James has so complicated the picture that this answer seems inadequate.

First, how can someone be expected to love another artificially? One does not create love purposefully. It is useless to imagine what "should" happen, that if he would have loved her (meaning he *should* have loved her) then all would be well. There is also the problem of May's saying that Marcher "will never consciously suffer." While Marcher does indeed suffer, it is perhaps for reasons other than the one May means. Endowed as she is by Marcher with sybil-like and sphynx-like qualities, she is also endowed with infinite wisdom by James, who narratively insists on her superior thinking throughout the story. The author favors May by never portraying her with irony; the reader has no reason to find fault with her. If she is right in her assumption that Marcher will never suffer, then Marcher is mistaken. He has not discovered his beast after all. Love for her was never there and never will be, from a fundamental "incapacity to function heterosexually" (Kaplan, 458). This suffering over lack of love for May is nothing to what remains concealed beneath the posturing of lost opportunities of heterosexual romance.

A possible answer for what the beast is comes in the images Marcher has created. His beast in the jungle must be approached without a lady; the reader is told that marriage is "out of the question." "Marcher's conviction, his apprehension, his obsession, in short, wasn't a privilege he could invite a woman to share; and that consequence of it was precisely what was the matter with him" (343). If no woman can fill that position, then perhaps, as May might well realize, only another man can fill the needed sexual quotient.

Eve Sedgwick contends that Marcher should have recognized his homosexuality. In her reading, Marcher "should" recognize the fullness of his sexuality both for his own satisfaction and for the relief of an attendant May, who sacrifices in excess of any personal reward. Sedgwick contends that May knows all along of Marcher's need to see his sexuality clearly in order to, in turn, see her as something other than "a terrifying demand or a devaluing complicity" (Sedgwick, "Beast in the Closet," 176). Of course, says Sedgwick, Marcher's discovery would also benefit himself. May would have him "progress from a vexed and gaping self-ignorance around his homosexual possibilities to a self-knowledge of them that would have freed him to find and enjoy a sexuality of whatever sort emerged" (Sedgwick, 177). Sedgwick sees Marcher as swallowing whole the law of society, becoming then an "enforcer" of society's code, imprisoning both himself and May within the circumference of his ignorance.

Meanwhile, I favor those critics who are cognizant of the possible homosexuality of Marcher and are equally aware of the effects of the consciousness of one's sexuality. David Van Leer contends that a fully exposed view of one's homosexuality in James's era could prove deadly. Van Leer mentions the possible penalties that await the overly observant person of variant sexuality. Marcher's self-awareness of his homosexuality was "theoretically possible" but "socially suicidal" (Van Leer, "Beast of the Closet," 593). He continues, "Our understanding of the historical moment . . . show[s] the difficulty (perhaps the impossibility) of such a resolution." Unlike Sedgwick, who denounces Marcher's self-ignorance, Van Leer sees the necessity of self-ignorance for the marginal male's "political and epistemological self-preservation" (Van Leer, 593).

In agreement with Van Leer, I contend that Marcher succeeds rather than fails. His success is in avoiding the recognition of his problematic sexuality

in an era when to do so would likely mean annihilation, whether psychological or social. His imagination aids his deception by fabricating an extended
metaphor of the jungle and the hunt that finally reinforces his masculinity
while thoroughly eluding the destructive potential of sexual recognition.
James demonstrates the inherent complexity in a battle of fictions between
the self and a society with little tolerance for rebellion, favoring necessary
deception over psychic dissolution, and showing in Marcher the mixed
blessings of such a success.

3

Sexual Surprise

Considerable negative criticism of James and his fiction has arisen from the underlying assumption that James and his fictional characters *chose* their sexual activity or lack thereof. Yet James and his characters had little choice when examined in the context of the "punitive authority" that governed sexuality and morality in the Victorian Age (Van Leer, "Beast of the Closet," 593). Alternatives to heterosexual matrimony were rarely if ever the topics of polite conversation, and those individuals who indulged in alternative sexual behaviors were severely punished if discovered.[1]

James "failed" to display sexuality because his survival in society depended upon subterfuge. He knew all too well the absurd consequences of acting in a sexually deviant manner in the Victorian Age, where society trapped the individual who could not adequately and aggressively pursue heterosexual marriage as his or her sexual aim. As one critic has said of Marcher in "The Beast in the Jungle," so might it be said of James that his uncertainty in the field of action "seems less self-ignorance than political and epistemological self-preservation" (Van Leer, 593). James concealed his sexuality because to do otherwise meant facing inevitable consequences.

James lived in a time when the difference between life and death was exactly the difference between thought and deed. In the decades preceding World War I, society would not have punished the "looks and language of homo-eroticism," unless these mildly suggestive acts were "incontrovertibly linked to homosexual activity" (Seymour, *Ring of Conspirators*, 187). What Victorians and Edwardians found objectionable was the act itself. If discovered, homosexuality "was treated as a criminal act to be punished with imprisonment and social ostracism."

The two or three centuries preceding the time of Henry James witnessed a growing intolerance of same-sex relationships. Homosexuality being a nonconcept before 1869, the relevant law concerned buggery, and dated from the 1530s; until 1861 it carried the maximum penalty of death (Weeks, "Inverts," 215). Other male homosexual acts were grouped under the heading "conspiracy to commit the major offense." A law that attempted to address these "other homosexual acts" was notoriously difficult to enforce, due to the law's ambiguity. The problem of enforcement was addressed in 1885 with Henry Labouchere's Criminal Law Amendment of 1885, which redefined homosexual acts as any "acts of gross indecency" between two men in public or private, to be charged as misdemeanors punishable by up to two years' hard labor. This amendment was followed by the 1898 Vagrancy Act, which stated that any male who solicited for immoral purposes was to be considered a "rogue and a vagabond." In 1912, the sentence for such indecent acts was set at six months' imprisonment with flogging for the second offense. "Although obviously less severe than a death sentence or life imprisonment for buggery, the new clauses were all-embracing and more effectively applied." In short, "all male homosexual activities were illegal between 1885 and 1967 in England" (Weeks, 215-16).

Nonetheless, sexual deviance flourished in Victorian times. In his discussions of sexuality, Freud argued that because the only biological aim of sex is the propagation of the species, even the ritual known as heterosexual courtship must be considered a perversion of the basic sexual act, often competing with and overshadowing coitus altogether. Freud writes, "No healthy person, it appears, can fail to make some addition that might be called perverse to the normal sexual aim; and the universality of this finding is in itself enough to show how inappropriate it is to use the word perversion as a term of reproach" (Freud, *Reader*, 253). The Victorians cultivated a variety of behaviors that delayed and sometimes distracted from basic sexual intercourse, transforming into an art the practice of perversion. "The clashes of social styles, pressures of temperament, neurotic inhibitions or proclivities, the anarchic charm of infatuation, made for variety in patterns of respectable love, sometimes for surprises" (Gay, *Bourgeois Experience*, vol. 2, 3). One account tells of a member of the bourgeoisie who epitomized the practice of delaying sexual gratification in return for alternative pleasure. The account reveals the young man's reluctance to marry the woman he was courting even when the woman's father not only granted the beloved's hand in marriage but insisted upon it. The suitor's greatest pleasure came from the passionate dreams he had of his beloved accompanied by the thought that he might never have her. Now that he found he could have her, he saw the woman's father as "threatening to deprive him of his only excuse for not marrying the girl he professed to love and dreamt of practically every night" (Gay, vol. 2, 13).

This young man's pleasure typifies the pleasure of the Victorian bachelor who finds alternative satisfactions. Curiously, bachelors garnered great respect while failing to achieve the *stated* aim of society, marriage. Perhaps society was content to imagine that these bachelors weren't having sex at all: asexuality posed no immediate threat to morality. In actuality, bachelorhood was yet another perversion from the celebrated aim of a heterosexual society, which was to have children and raise them in the security of a family setting.

Other "perversions" of the sexual aim were cultivated in Victorian society. Sexual pleasure could be found in music, food, nature, and religion. The Victorian Age loved the fetish, where an intense yet private pleasure could be found in an unexpected object of desire. Some documentation exists for the eroticization of the very symbols of the age, such as in the pleasure of observing or riding on a powerful steel locomotive, or enjoying a day of conspicuous consumption in a gigantic department store. "Nineteenth-century middle-class culture swarmed with exceptions" to the sexual norm (Gay, vol. 2, 100).

Why such variety in an apparent age of sexual repression? The answer may lie in the question itself. Repression encouraged deviation, the channeling of energy into avenues not readily censored. The supreme social rule was reticence (Gay, vol. 2, 203). So long as the pleasant surface of respectability was maintained, the individual could revel in secret pleasures. The effect was to make the nineteenth century "the age of multiplication: a dispersion of sexualities, a strengthening of their disparate forms, a multiple implantation of 'perversions'" (Foucault, *History of Sexuality*, 1:37).[2]

Perhaps even more revolutionary was the emergence of an open discussion of sexuality among the intelligentsia. Discussion of sex became a distinguishing feature of the bourgeoisie: "It was in the 'bourgeois' or 'aristocratic' family that the sexuality of children and adolescents was first problematized, and feminine sexuality medicalized; [they] were the first to be alerted to the potential pathology of sex. . . . It was this family that first became a locus for the psychiatrization of sex" (Foucault, *History of Sexuality*, 1:120). Discussion of sexual behavior so distinguished the Victorian Age from earlier eras to belie any repression of sexuality at all. Academics began to formulate a *scientia sexualis* to label all manner of deviations. Far from silencing talk of sexuality, "authorities" on human sexuality aimed to define any and all deviant forms of sexual expression, to talk about these behaviors and compel their patients to "confess" illicit activities. There was nothing less than "an institutional incitement to speak about [sex], and to do so more and more; a determination on the part of agencies of power to hear it spoken about, and to cause *it* to speak through explicit articulation and endlessly accumulated detail" (Foucault, *History of Sexuality*, 1:18). Terms like "invert" and "homosexual," "voyeur" and "pedant," "fetish" and "necrophile" entered academic discourse at this time, clinically validating age-old behaviors and so giving society a new way to think and talk about such behavior. By way of example, the concept of homosexuality as it is known today did not exist before the late 1800s. The term "sodomite" in common parlance had historically encompassed all same-sex relations, and was often confused with pederasty. Once the term "homosexual,"coined by Karoly Maria Benhart in 1869, was adopted, scholars could codify patterns of sexual behavior, as well as a lifestyle that may or may not include the sexual act itself. (Weeks, 226). Carl Westphal's *Archiv für Neurologie* (1870) participated in this academic foment, treating homosexuality (what he called a "contrary sexual sensation") as something far more complex than the act itself, "more a sexual sensibility than a type of sexual relations."[3]

One of the most notable writers on sexuality in the late nineteenth century was the celebrated sexologist Richard von Krafft-Ebing, whose *Psychopathic Sexualis* brought him "fame, controversy, and continuous demand for revised editions" (Weeks, 223). Krafft-Ebing's prestige in the European university community encouraged other scholars "both to write and read freely" on the once taboo subject of sexuality. He led the way in legitimizing sexuality as a topic for discussion and made sensitive subjects like homosexuality worthy of "dispassionate investigation." Nevertheless, Krafft-Ebing was quick to consign sexual "heresies" such as homosexuality to the "domain of mental pathology" (Weeks, 229). Meanwhile, Havelock Ellis attracted attention with his "explosive book" *Sexual Inversion* (Weeks, 232). Unlike Krafft-Ebing, who tended to brood over sexuality, Ellis manifested great pleasure in his discussions, particularly of sexual abnormalities, obsessed as he was with finding "the many and varied gratifications that sexual inclinations can devise" (Gay, vol. 2, 231).

William James contributed to these discussions of sexuality, though he is now deemed a "somewhat prim spokesman" on the subject (Myers, *William James*, 212). He "vehemently" opposed the libido theory of nature and disagreed with Charles Mercer's theory that suicide could be linked to sexual activity. William also read Henry Flinch, whose notion he rebutted that "romantic love is a late product of evolution" (Myers, 427). He corresponded directly with Havelock Ellis, whose works he had read. Not always in agreement, William James wrote to Ellis, "I think you too indulgent to that monster of meanness, Casanova" (Myers, 213). Havelock Ellis makes reference to William James in a rather obscure passage from his *Psychology of Sex*: "A partial contribution to the analysis of modesty has been made by Professor James, who, with his usual insight and lucidity, has set forth certain of its characteristics" (Myers, 533).

With William involved directly in these discussions, Henry as younger brother also spoke out, through the subtle medium of fiction. Yet where language helped Henry acquire a polite distance from this sensitive topic in public, in private his sexuality compelled him to live out what others only talked about.

As a prominent citizen, Henry James no doubt pondered the question of how to derive sexual pleasure and yet maintain respectability in a world where desire often led to despair. James was not one to subvert openly the status quo. This task he left to the thick-skinned, such as Walt Whitman, whose lines James read on occasion to enraptured audiences (Edel, *Henry James*, 599). Not all humanity has the energy to come to terms with the demands of egalitarian love as Whitman did.[4] Unlike Whitman, in his life and art Henry James appears to have quietly sought the sexual spaces that the status quo overlooked. The key for James was individual satisfaction, not the megalomaniacal insistence on a new world order. His exploration into the world of sexual pleasure appears rather as a "permutation" of the "familiar set of relations of power and exchange" (Martin, "Knights Errant," 201).

However, simply to write fiction in the varied artistic movements of the Victorian Age meant in part to vary from the norm of earnestness and stern morality. Much of what James wrote may be seen as a subtle representation of aestheticism. Jonathan Freedman in his *Professions of Taste* aligns James with a moderate aestheticism that to a lesser degree participated in the subversion of sexual mores acted out in the more radical aestheticism of Pater, Wilde, and others. In Freedman's reading, James's fiction promotes an "austere aestheticism" more accessible to American audiences that nonetheless presents a subtle protest "against the sexual mores of Victorian England" (Freedman, *Professions*, 2). Characters like Ralph Touchett and Lambert Strether each in their own way typify the marginal, effete, imaginative-more-than-participatory aesthete who artistically shapes alternatives to the social norm—variations on themes and types worked out by the very artists James would often and contradictorily condemn for their decadence, but with whom he had much in common. His borrowings from aestheticism identify James as a quasi-revolutionary, reenforcing his position at the sexual margins of society.

James early on departed from the norm in a strange debilitation known as his "obscure hurt." This "wound," both psychological and physical, preceded a life apart from the sexual norm. One effect of this difference was his puritanical renunciation of the discussion of sex, which persuaded several scholars to stereotype James as a prude. Indeed he characteristically avoided discussion of delicate matters, as at the breakfast table at Lamb House, where he once silenced Violet Hunt's discussion of the "subject of passion" by pointing in horror to a portrait of his mother (Seymour, 96). James tolerated the subject of sex only when he could trust that the participants would exercise the utmost discretion, finding in Hunt the "very soul of indiscretion" (Seymour, 147).

This propriety was countered by an intense desire that lived beneath the surface, undermining categorization of James as asexual. James quietly and consistently cultivated a fabric of human relationships that addressed his sexual desire within the limits of propriety. Whereas Oscar Wilde and others would leap into the abyss of scandal headlong, James safely skirted the edge, exploring in life and fiction the possibilities society left for marginal figures like himself.

James strayed from the norm in his relations with both men and women. As was mentioned earlier, among his most frequently mentioned relations with women are those with his cousin Minnie Temple and his friends Edith Wharton and Constance Fenimore Woolson. One source contends that "insofar as James was ever in love with a woman, he was in love with his witty, charming cousin Minnie" (Seymour, 169). This relationship succeeded in part because it did not demand sexual intimacy; James could enjoy a degree of eroticism apart from heterosexual conventions: "She had been a Diana in the temple of his life" (Edel, 5:409).

With adulthood James saw a possible corruption of their innocent affair if Minnie should choose to marry. However, Minnie died of tuberculosis at age twenty-five, allowing James to perpetuate her innocence and youth. Henry wrote to his sister-in-law Alice that Minnie in life allowed him to worship her from afar as the "very heroine of our common scene," while in death she allowed him to pay homage to "a steady unfaltering luminary in the mind," rather than "a flickering wasting earth-stifled lamp." Henry explained to William what ravages their cousin had been saved from by her death: "The more I think of her the more perfectly satisfied I am to have her translated from this changing realm of fact to the steady realm of thought" (quoted in Seymour, 169-70). Henry seemed "almost to welcome her death because he could take total possession of her in his mind and memory" (Edel, 5:110), and afterward secured her innocence with his imagination, enjoying a relationship that was now incontestably platonic.

The possibility of alternative and compensatory pleasures became a trademark in James's life—he would aim for the maximum of eroticism just short of physicality. His friendship with Edith Wharton has been described as "not physical but inescapably erotic" (Powers, *James and Wharton*, 13). Wharton used the words "intimate" and "marriage" to convey the closeness of their friendship. In the sense of a "marriage of true minds," she thought of James as "perhaps the most intimate friend" she ever had (quoted in Seymour, 235), saying of him after his death, "The love of my life died today, and I with him" (quoted in Seymour, 254). While Wharton and James apparently never engaged in physical intimacy, they enjoyed a mental intimacy tinged with eroticism, fortified by their mutual realization of the impossibility of any conventional romance. It is in this field that James played most capably.

Constance Fenimore Woolson fit less comfortably into James's interpretation of the erotic. While he contented himself with friendship, the woman known to James as "Fenimore" longed for physical intimacy and the possibility of marriage. Perhaps at no other time was James's sexual difference displayed so prominently as in this conflict with heterosexual expectation. Woolson died tragically "in a moment of high fever during influenza" in 1894, leaving her friend to wonder if he had perhaps played a role in her untimely death (Edel, 4:147), which persisted in his memory as a painful reminder of a role he could never fill to her expectations. He cared for her but felt threatened by the fact that—unlike Edith Wharton, who had other men in her life who filled romantic longings—Woolson, reclusive by nature, appeared to want only him. He imagined her after death as a loving, suffocating, nightmarish presence that would drag him into the world of the dead if he let it, assigned as he was to the task of dealing with her personal effects, among these a quantity of "funereal black" dresses that he decided could best be disposed of by drowning them in the Venice lagoon nearby. Accounts report that "he threw [the dresses] into the water and they came up like balloons all around him, and the more he tried to throw them down, they got all this air, the more they came up and he was surrounded by these horrible black balloons. . . . He tried to beat these horrible black things down and up they came again and he was surrounded by them" (quoted in Kaplan, 386). The world of women could please him best from a distance.

James's other fascination was for the world of men—not in terms of finance and scholarship, or drinking at pubs and rubbing shoulders and brawling, but in terms of eroticism. As Fred Kaplan discloses in his recent biography of James, beginning in the mid-1890s James established several intimate relationships; "in each case, he fell in love with a younger man" (Kaplan, *Henry James*, 402). He did so, says Kaplan, in order to "be flexible, to be open to emotional interaction, to 'only live' in the sense of being true to his own desires and needs, difficult as they were to identify" (Kaplan, 401). The letters he sent to these young men demonstrate a passion that on occasion matches the most torrid correspondence of Victorian and Edwardian times. His well of loneliness knew no bounds on those occasions when it could be unleashed in the safety of private correspondence.

While James could deny the sex act itself, hugs and kisses and proclamations of passion came in profusion. Documentation of his "courting" of males appears most frequently later in his life, after years of experience had taught him what would be exacted as payment for his pleasures, and in turn what pleasures could be had for free. He discovered that the penalties were small for an aging bachelor's verbal appreciation of a younger man's physical beauty. In 1899, on a visit to his friend Mary Augusta Ward in Italy, James observed the breathtaking splendor of the countryside, the ruins of villas, the freshness of a blue Alban lake, and the charms of a particular Italian youth. Ward wrote of James's obvious fascination with the boy, "straight and lithe and handsome as a young Bacchus." She recalled James approaching the boy, who stood among some ancient ruins. He struck up a conversation, walking beside him and listening to his chatter. Ward recorded that for some time after the incident James repeated the youth's name, Aristodemo, over and over as if he were caressing the boy himself (Seymour, 187).

James's homoerotic tendencies can be traced back perhaps to his sibling attachment to William, and at least as far back as 1860, when the young Henry discovered his cousin Gus Barker posing nude for brother William and art teacher William Morris Hunt, boasting a "perfect gymnastic figure." Young Henry admired both his brother's drawing of Barker's figure and, perhaps more so, the model himself (Kaplan, 47). His feelings for men intensified over the years in a slow, steady stream of reluctant revelations, such as his sentiments for Paul Joukowsky, with whom James "briefly fell in love" in 1876 (Kaplan, 171). Always James's rush of feelings for men was matched by the swift censorship of fear of retaliation, as with his feelings for Joukowsky, which subsided partly because of his discovery of an alliance with the Wagner entourage, whose flagrant homosexuality frightened and disgusted him. James's response to the Wagner following predicted his reaction to Oscar Wilde's flaunting of homosexuality, which he found disgusting because it was threatening. James saw in these openly gay men the terrifying visage of himself run amuck against social codes that guaranteed retaliation, most likely in the form of ignominy and imprisonment.[5]

One way to respond to the gap between homosexual thought and homosexual act was to live a double life, as James witnessed voyeuristically in John Addington Symonds, whom he met in 1877. While James confined his homosexuality to thoughts and mild acts of affection such as hugs and kisses, Symonds acted on his homosexuality during the years that he was married with children. Suddenly, in the early 1880s, Symonds left his double life with his wife and daughters, compelled by his "Victorian need to rescue homosexuality from sinfulness by associating it with ideal Greek values" (Kaplan, 301). From that time on, he wrote and spoke openly on the subject of homosexuality as it had affected the Classical Age. As much as he detested Wilde and Joukowsky, James admired Symonds for his complex response to homosexuality, first in a quiet double life, and then in an openness not characterized by reckless abandon but by a mature wish to change society.

James also sought change, but quietly, and first of all in himself. He too knew the pains of a double life, not in marriage but in the psychological struggle between the self that recognized the dual appeals of society and sexuality. Kaplan draws an interesting connection between James's aging and expanding flesh and his expanding awareness of missed sexual opportunities. James's "expanding flesh implied the sensuality that he had repressed; it was a reminder of the powerfulness of pleasure, of expansive eroticism" (Kaplan, 298). While the weight brought on by a slowing metabolism and quickened appetite dashed any hopes of eternal youth, the awareness of his body perhaps terrified him the more from inattention than from excess feeding. How could sensuality and sexuality be recovered in his mature years after suppression in the very years that had expected appeasement?

It was in the midst of his struggle between self and society that James gathered to himself in the twenty or so years before his death a group of young men who aroused his passion. Though James is known for his lack of physical intimacy, this is true only in the most limited sense, for he expressed his passion through hugs and kisses rather than through the sex act. Gaillard Lapsley and Arthur Benson once discussed their mutual friendship with James. Benson reports:

> Lapsley said, "If I had caught [James] in my arms, kissed his cheeks, as I have often done, it would be all right"—this power of receiving caresses is a new light to me on H.J.—he lives in an atmosphere of hugging—that is probably the secret of Hugh Walpole's success, the kisses of youth—he [James] is jaded by the slobbering osculations of elderly men with false teeth. (quoted in Seymour, 188)

James loved beautiful young men as an artist loves an exquisitely sculpted human form, as in his appreciation of the young Hendrik Andersen. "When they were together it was Andersen's stature, his shoulders, his arms and hands, the solid physical presence that counted" (Edel, 5:103). Andersen dreamed of sculpting male beauty in statues reminiscent of Michelangelo's *David*. James praised the artwork of Andersen much as he would have wished to verbally express affection for Andersen. Andersen sent a terra cotta bust of the Conte Alberto Bevilacqua to James as a gift. The older man placed the bust in a prominent spot in the dining room and reported to Andersen sometime later, "I've struck up a tremendous intimacy with dear little Conte Alberto, and we literally can't live without each other" (quoted in Seymour, 189).

Andersen at one point was commissioned to sculpt a nude, but the statue was dismissed finally on charges of obscenity. James wrote in words of consolation, "What a dismal doom for a sculptor to work for a great vulgar stupid community that revels in every hideous vulgarity and only quakes at the clean and blessed nude—the last refuge of Honour" (quoted in Edel, 5:102). James never tired of talking with Andersen about art, however mundane these talks might have seemed to the outsider. "Nothing sounds banal to the lover, and [James] was in love" (Seymour, 189).

James also accepted the company of the young Hugh Walpole. Whereas Andersen was emotionally unbalanced, Walpole satisfied James's desire for more stability with his consistently cheerful demeanor, and while not his intellectual equal, Walpole had a sense of wit. Their relationship encompassed "a great deal of laughter." Walpole loved James as the greatest person he had ever known: "Beyond equal. I cannot speak about him" (quoted in Seymour, 192). To James, Walpole was the younger man in need of a mentor, his "belovedest little Hugh," "beloved boy," and "darling little Hugh," feeling for "the delightful and interesting young Hugh Walpole . . . the tenderest sympathy and an absolute affection" (quoted in Edel, 5:401, 403).

It has been rumored that Walpole offered himself physically to James, but sources claim that James answered Walpole's advances with, "I can't. I can't" (quoted in Seymour, 195). He apparently considered discretion the best choice, after a life of gazing at the wide gulf that separated desire from action in a world where respectability held a premium. James's yearnings were "more passionately expressed in words and looks than in actions" (Seymour, 187). His letters were his way of making love, as in a letter to Morton Fullerton, where James writes, "My difficulty is that I love you too much. . . . You touch and penetrate me to the quick, and I can only stretch out my hand to draw you closer" (*Letters*, 4:453).

Late in life, James befriended another young man, Jocelyn Persse, who would be of the three perhaps his greatest love. James once said to Walpole of Persse, "I not only love him—I *love* to love him" (quoted in Edel, 5:408). "Whether the homo-erotic feeling between Persse and James was 'acted out' is perhaps less important than the fact that a great state of affection existed between them" (Edel, 5:190). Their relationship was of the tenderest nature, with James deeply in love with the blond and gregarious thirty-year-old man. While Persse was not intellectual, he possessed a gift for gab and an ease about life that James could not resist. James told Persse, "The record of your eternal Bacchanalia (do you know what Bacchanalia are?) continues to excite my vague envy" (quoted in Edel, 5:186). "If James felt lonely, he could rely on Persse to come rushing down to London to cheer him with a jolly evening" (Seymour, 196).

James also took pleasure in the company of his longtime friend Howard Sturgis. Though their friendship reveals no explicit sexuality, Sturgis satisfied in James the need for a man who would not act as other men do. What James occasionally missed in his companionship with men was the womanly influence, but in androgynous form. Sturgis offered this ambiguity, wandering between masculinity and femininity with his flair for domesticity. "Howard Sturgis believed that there was nothing women did that men could not do better" (Edel, 5:193). James's companion could embroider and knit with skill. "He would sit with his thick golden hair—which later became silvered—beautifully brushed, his small feet daintily crossed, in the middle of a square carpet on the lawn, or by his fireside, with his basket, his dogs about him, working on some large golden-threaded design" (Edel, 5:193).

James knew much more about sexual desire and its expression than is often attributed to him. In respect to sexuality, James mastered his actions but ultimately could not deny his objects of desire, which contradicted the aims of heterosexual courtship and marriage. Society expected of him that he marry or at least reveal some passionate attachment to a woman. The *New York Evening Journal* (January 4, 1906) contained a caricature of Henry James, with the caption "Henry James and his Shrine: This is the celebrated author, reported to be in love with Emilie Grigsby, who is Mildred Theale, heroine of his novel *The Wings of a Dove*, whom he describes in terms of adoration, had placed on a pedestal as an object of adoration, an image of Miss Grigsby." The paper continued with an article that pressed the issue of marriage: "It may or may not be true that Henry James was, as report has stated of him, at one time deeply in love with Emilie Grigsby—that at sixty-five he sneered at conventionalities and in full knowledge of her past laid his great fame at her young feet and asked her to marry him." Society intended to apply the formula of courtship and marriage to this author.

However, if one can trust the accounts of his intimates, intentions of marriage probably never existed for him. James's sexuality was of a different and in some ways surprising nature. His road would necessarily be that of "substitutions and compensations" (Kaplan, 54), where pleasure would be in the discovery of exactly what he could "get away with." James sought late in life to recover those physical satisfactions linked with eroticism and sexuality that would let him feel what others felt, just short of the sexual act itself, writing in *The Ambassadors* that one must live with "sufficient intensity" to provide oneself with "what may be called excitement" (Edel, 5:70). Words, hugs, kisses, ecstasies of the imagination—these would fill his quotient of eroticism.

In his fiction, James created a world of sexual surprise defined by Foucault as "peripheral sexualities," where possibility reigns over mundane reality. His artistic works provide glimpses of alternative sexual desire and expression, collectively attending to the sexual uncertainty in the author's life.

James knew that what the world would expect of him would be expected of his art, an unswerving devotion to heterosexual romance. The bulk of Western literature had focused on the amorous courtship between men and women. The imaginations of most Victorian readers pointed to marriage; "the young men and women whose emotional encounters most [nineteenth-century] fictions charted could navigate the perilous seas of love only to steer at length into the safe harbor of marriage. . . . Most readers expected, and normally got, nothing less" than a novel ending in matrimony (Foucault, "Sexual Choice," 18-19). Even writers of great subtlety frequently submitted to the easy climax of marital bliss in order to satisfy an insatiably heterosexual audience. George Eliot's chapter of *Adam Bede* entitled "Marriage Bells" offers one example (Gay, vol. 2, 143). By the time of James, heterosexuality had become "a well-known tale" told to consumers of fiction who expected nothing less than "family, kinship, and marriage" (DuPlessis, *Writing Beyond*, 1). Because the bulk of Western literature paid homage to courtship leading to marriage, James would have had to follow suit in order to win the respect of his readers.

Superficially, James's works pay homage to heterosexual courtship. The bulk of his fiction consists of intricate relations between males and females, all hopefully leading to marriage. However, as has been lamented frequently by some critics, James generally avoids illustrations of happy courtship and marriage, with the possible exception of his last finished novel, *The Golden Bowl*. One critic laments that James showed little fondness for the "right to be happy," as demonstrated in his favoring "genderless minds usually devoid of desire, who discover the secret shameful facts of life about a species essentially alien" (Habegger, *Gender*, 255). Another critic bemoans James's failure in his later fiction to portray a character who can achieve the "pleasure of fulfilled and consummated desires." Instead, the author gives the reader only "monomaniacal" characters whose actions are "deleterious for others in the external world," as they suggest "a horror of intimacy, of sexuality" (Przybylowicz, *Desire and Repression*, 24, 37).

One source of concern is James's sentiments regarding marriage. He once wrote, "One's attitude toward marriage is a fact—the most characteristic part doubtless of one's attitude toward life. If I were to marry I should be guilty in my own eyes of inconsistency—I should pretend to think quite a little better of life than I really do" (*Letters*, 2:314). One critic recently expressed horror at this "remarkable if rather appalling admission" of James's attitude concerning marriage and recommended that "one ought to approach the theme of love in Henry James within a broad context of ethical and ontological, as well as psychological concerns" (McWhirter, *Desire and Love*, 4).

Another source of difficulty in James's work is the narrative's refusal to eroticize overt references to heterosexual activity. Admittedly, James's work abounds with examples of heterosexual romance, notably in the extramarital affairs of Maisie's parents in *What Maisie Knew*, the affairs of Kate Croy and Merton Densher in *The Wings of the Dove* and Charlotte Stant and the Prince in *The Golden Bowl*, and the sexual intimacy between Madame de Vionnet and Chad Newsome in *The Ambassadors*. Despite numerous examples of sexual activity, however, the erotic component is almost invariably denied at the moment the affair is named. Often information about a sexual affair is circumscribed by the psychological limitations of the character whose vision dominates the story, as in the cases of Maisie and Strether. Only in *The Wings of the Dove* and *The Golden Bowl* is eroticism readily evoked, and even then passion is censored by an elegant decorum (Edel, 5:113). As Adeline Tintner suggests, in James's fiction there is no sexual liaison as in the typical case of the French "concealed attachment"; there are no "paraphernalia of conceal-ment" in preparation for the "drama of alarm and exposure" (Tintner, *Cosmopolitan World*, 253).[6] James's work appears driven by a motive of purity that separates named instances of heterosexual passion from their full erotic potential. As James wrote to Howard Sturgis in 1899, there is nothing "so indelicate as a bed!" (quoted in Kaplan, 454).

To find eroticism in James's work, one might need to search elsewhere. A surprising degree of eroticism can be found in instances of *marginal* sexual behavior: while he avoided the subject of heterosexual intercourse (what he called "the great relation"), he nurtured the "secret, one-sided passion" (Tintner, 248). Eroticism in such instances plays off the impulse to censor such activities. Linda S. Boren argues in *Eurydice Reclaimed* that much of James's work, particularly that written in his later style, has as its foundation a "desire to elude censorship" (Boren, 23). Where one cannot specify, for fear of punishment, one can safely *suggest*. As Barthes has written, conceal-ment eroticizes the subject. It is as if James is "getting away" with something wrong. He felt that his province as a writer included all subjects, many of which were unjustifiably forbidden: "The province of art is . . . all experience. That is a sufficient answer to those who maintain that it must not touch the bad things of life, who stick into its divine unconscious bosom little prohibitory inscriptions on the end of stick, such as we see in public gardens—'It is forbidden to walk on the grass; it is forbidden to touch the flowers; it is forbidden' " ("Art of Fiction," 17). Indeed he not only imagined such censorship; society on occasion confirmed his suspicions. In 1891, he watched the editor of *The Century* turn down his short story "The Pupil" for reasons of decency. In 1896, James was forced to withdraw a critical review of Alexandre Dumas when *The Century* again considered his work "indecent" (Kaplan, 410). He favored subtlety, staging a game of hide-and-seek, but not child's play, for his subject hides not only because he wants to but because he must. The fun never ends, for James's readers can search only with their imaginations, endlessly played out on the wavelength of the erotic where at bottom they may find something, but always a distortion, and never the thing itself.

Psychoanalysis contends that art is a repression of sexual fantasies beneath a surface of "condensation and displacement" (Przybylowicz, 6). In psychoanalytic theory, the writer unconsciously defers the sexual fantasy in order to render the artistic work acceptable to both artist and public: the artist "bribes us by the purely formal—that is, aesthetic—yield of his pleasure which he offers us in the presentation of his phantasies" (Freud, *Reader*, 443). Art does this for two reasons: First, to expose marginal behaviors would no doubt repel readers who themselves depend on repression of their own desires in order to function as social beings: "such phantasies, when we learn them, repel us or at least leave us cold" (Freud, 443). Second, the sublimation of sexual fantasy beneath form promises its own rewards. In this process of delayed gratification, art finds its parallel in the process leading to sexual gratification: "We give the name of an *incentive bonus*, or a *fore-pleasure*, to a yield of pleasure such as this [of art]" (Freud, 443). The artist suppresses immediate gratification for alternative yields.

Indeed, eroticism depends on concealment. In his *Camera Lucida*, Roland Barthes uses photographs to show that eroticism derives in part from the concealment of the potentially erotic subject. He distinguishes the erotic from the pornographic by stressing the necessary presence of clothing, for example, to conceal and thereby eroticize the human figure. Without this concealment, the subject would enter the realm of the pornographic where nothing is left to the imagination. Barthes suggests that the eroticized subject "is a pornographic [subject] that has been disturbed, fissured," often by means of partial concealment. Erotic art gives the viewer what the pornographic cannot, a certain "punctum," as Barthes calls it, thus differentiated from mundane pornography. The erotic shuns wholeness; there is "nothing more homogeneous" than pornography, says Barthes (*Camera Lucida*, 41).

James's style at times eroticizes its marginal subject by means of ellipsis, a literary means of concealment. So much remains unsaid that the reader is left groping for a complete image. According to Jacques Lacan, all language is born of lack, representing a rupture between what the speaker wishes to say and what is finally communicated. Language inherently fails to say all; rather it offers distortion. Far from resisting this lack in language, James submits to and even seeks "deficiency" by means of ellipsis, at times eroticizing his subject or, as in Roland Barthes's example of an erotic photograph, partially covering the naked article.

Often ellipsis has decorum as its aim. The rupture between the "libidinous urges of the body and the repressiveness of decorum" is a telltale sign of erotic literature (Boren, 22). In such literature, far from attempting open expression of the "real article," the language decorously moves away from the thing itself, straining the reader's perceptions by distorting the image and thus heightening the erotic component.

Take for example an elliptical scene in *The Ambassadors*, in which the element of ellipsis renders the images incomplete, thus distorting the final picture. Certain elements are emphasized—they are enlarged, bordering on the grotesque. The passage referred to comes early in the novel and evokes the erotic element in part from its setting. Strether and Waymarsh are preparing to bed down for the night in a room of a London hotel. Every image that the reader receives of Waymarsh comes through Strether's consciousness, and the images Strether offers up are distorted and incomplete. All the reader sees of Waymarsh are bits and pieces: "The occupant of the bed thrust so far a pair of slippered feet that the visitor has almost to step over them in his recurrent rebounds from his chair to fidget back and forth" (*Ambassadors*, 30). The figure in bed looks "unnaturally big and black." Here are two men in what is apparently a very small room, suggesting a forced intimacy between two people who have not "at home, during years before this sudden brief and almost bewildering reign of comparative ease, found so much as a day for a meeting" (30).

The sudden intimacy is almost unbearable for Strether—unbearable because it is uncomfortable, and uncomfortable because of the risk involved. That the narrator and Strether interpret the scene as dangerous is suggested by the extreme gentleness of the language, which describes Strether as a womanly "nurse" for "a large snubbed child" as he assists Waymarsh into bed. The process of getting into bed is described both delicately and suggestively as a "consummation" where Strether, "with a kind of coercive hand for it," assists Waymarsh, who happens to be feeling a bit of a "prostration." With "smaller touches" and a "sufficiency of blanket," the process gives Strether no small sense of "indulgence." Waymarsh comments to Strether in the interim, "You're a very attractive man." Strether gives a final "twitch to his companion's blanket" after he has "hovered in vague pity" over the bed and then "gains the door." After some discussion about Strether and Mrs. Newsome, Waymarsh cries out, "Well, *I* won't marry you!" "Neither, when it comes to that—" Strether answers. He escapes through the door, laughing (not unlike a maiden escaping the clutches of a suitor).

While it is often the language, at once "impossibly innocent or embarrass-ingly explicit" (Kaplan, 406), that effects eroticism in James's fiction, so too his characters are sometimes the vehicles of eroticism. Sexually ambivalent characters like Lambert Strether evoke eroticism in the tension they create between sexual norms and their abnormal longing. The gaze of the marginal male is a distracted one, seeming to fix on the idol of normality but all the while drifting to the horizon of abnormality.

In an atmosphere of secrecy, James invites his marginal characters to explore their desires safely. One mode of exploration that he allows such characters is the fetish. Walter Anderson argues that most of James's oeuvre is "an art of veiling obsessional subjects" (Anderson, "Visiting Mind," 528). James's interest in the fetish, evidenced in his writing as early as 1878, is perhaps a "fictional variation of James's own sexual displacement, a man fixated with 'pretty things' that are essentially dead" (Kaplan, 212). In this he shares with his aestheticist contemporaries Wilde and Pater a fetishism that appears as a libidinal deflection from "normal outlets onto art objects" (Freedman, 149). The fetish as a form of obsession epitomizes a departure from the norm as it distracts the subject from the human element altogether, calling attention instead to an inanimate object or a particular body part. An insufficient interest in the "normal sexual aim" is thought to be the precon-dition of fetishism. What replaces the normal sex object is an object that, however much it might resemble the heterosexual norm, is "entirely unsuited" to serve procreation (Freud, 249). In truth much of humanity partake in fetishistic practices as they obsess on some particular attribute of a beloved. Common fetishist objects are fur, women's stockings, women's shoes, women's gloves, and especially women's underpants. Fetishism may include visual enjoyment of the article or it may insist upon physical contact by "fondling, kissing, and smelling" the object (Bootzin, *Abnormal Psychology,* 324).

Krafft-Ebing in 1886 reported a case of fetishism where Mr. X satisfied himself on his wedding night by "running his fingers through the wealth of [his wife's] tresses." Two nights later, Mr. X produced "an immense wig, with enormously long hair" and requested that his wife wear it. Apparently Mr. X's sexual desire depended on his wife's wearing such a wig, for thereafter when Mrs. X "removed the wig she lost at once all charm for her husband."

The result of this marriage after five years "was two children, and a collection of seventy-two wigs" (Bootzin, 324).

Though James produced no wigs as fetishes in his fictional works, he did allow his male characters to enjoy a preoccupation with physical objects to the exclusion of normative sexual interests. Fetishism suited James's sexually marginalized men, as it is typically a practice of males. Also, fetishism typified to much of Victorian society those marginal individuals owning a certain "biological inadequacy" who were compelled to practice not authentic sex, but one of its "frauds" (Foucault, *History of Sexuality*, 1:154).[7] In addition, and from a less cynical perspective, fetishism offers a nongenital source of pleasure: "the fetish object does not necessarily give sexual gratification in the genital sense." Rather fetishism can be defined as a "kind of adoration, a wish to possess or unite with, to appreciate with all the senses . . . the fetish object" (Gosselin, "Fetishism," 90).

While the fetishes in James's work fail to elicit overt sexual pleasure, these objects nonetheless distract from normal sexual practices to the point of obsession. One case involves Lambert Strether, who enjoys a singular fascination for women's clothing. Strether's arrival in Europe stirs up desires dormant during his Woollett years. His walks down the streets of London and Paris make him "want things [the reader is never told what precisely] that he shouldn't know what to do with. It was by the oddest, the least admissable of laws demoralising him now; and the way it boldly took was to make him want more wants." Strether sums up his early exploration of Europe as a "kind of finely lurid intimation of what one might find at the end of that process" (*Ambassadors*, 37). Then there is the episode of the velvet band, perhaps motivated by nothing more than his appreciation of Maria's appearance: "What was it but an uncontrolled perception that his friend's velvet band somehow added, in her appearance, to the value of every other item?" However, the issue is complicated by Strether's self-condemnation, as he finds the attraction "frivolous, no doubt idiotic, and above all unexpected." Rather than placing him comfortably in the world of men who desire women, the attraction to the article of clothing dislocates him, putting him at odds with normal masculine behavior: "What, certainly, had a man conscious of a man's work in the world to do with red velvet bands?" Instead of informing Strether's masculine ideal, he perceives his attraction to the band as a distraction. Rather than leading to the woman herself, the fetish distracts him by reminding him of other articles of clothing he has appreciated. He thinks of Mrs. Newsome's "black silk dress," a very "handsome" one, and of a certain ruche she used to wear. In the end, the whole episode with Maria Gostrey's velvet band strikes Strether as "vaguely pathetic; but there it all was, and pathetic was doubtless in the conditions the best thing it could possibly be" (43).

After considering for a time his married life, Strether is on this same evening distracted by other articles of clothing, identifying two characters in a play he is watching not by their acting abilities, but by their dress: the actress wears a yellow frock, the actor a "perpetual evening dress." He then thinks of Chad Newsome, and wonders if he too will wear a "perpetual evening dress" (44). Perhaps it is no accident that Strether thinks of himself much later in the novel as a dresser of dolls: after discovering (or uncovering) the embarrassing "nakedness" of Madame de Vionnet and Chad's affair, Strether "almost blushed, in the dark, for the way he had dressed the possibility in vagueness, as a little girl might have dressed her doll" (313). His fetish for clothing mirrors his concern for "dressing" the nakedness of sexual intimacy. In place of intimacy between a man and a woman, Strether appears to favor the distraction of pretty frocks and velvet bands; such a fetish is a safe alternative to more visible pleasures that would incriminate an aging widower.

Fetishism also plays a important role in *The Aspern Papers*. In this tale, the Aspern papers offer the unnamed protagonist-narrator's "fetishes of Aspern"; the letters represent "an ideal Aspern—a man whom the narrator considers a 'god'" (Person, "Eroticism and Creativity," 21). The narrator desires the inanimate object over any conventional sexual interest. "Instead of investing in a relationship outside the self, James's narrator directs his attention and energy at such an introjected object, a fetish of Jeffrey Aspern he himself has composed from his research" (Person, 21). The narrator concedes that Jeffrey Aspern's papers are "very necessary" to his "happiness," admitting that the collection of Aspern's papers "diverts me more than I can say."

In order to portray the Aspern papers as a distraction from other love interests, James creates a male character thoroughly alienated from marriage and family. The "sociability, of cousinship and family life" is "queer" to this character (*Aspern Papers*, 248). He prefers to observe the "splendid common domicile, familiar, domestic, and resonant," from the safety of the gallery (249).

The narrator alienates himself from women by dehumanizing them with language, referring to Miss Juliana as a witch, an old lady, and a "sarcastic, profane, cynical old woman" (202), a "relic" discarded at the death of Jeffrey Aspern (162). She is but a shred of "esoteric knowledge" that will lead him to his true object of desire (181). As for Miss Tita, she is merely a stand-in for the Aspern papers; the narrator courts her only in attempted consummation of his lust for the papers of Jeffrey Aspern. He calls her a "poor deluded, infatuated, extravagant lady" (246) and a "ridiculous old woman" (250). The world of literature that he so adores leaves no room for such women, or any women for that matter: he believes firmly that Jeffrey Aspern is "no doubt not a woman's poet" (155). When Aspern had consented to write of women, the narrator acknowledges that he would have written of these "Maenads" with far less compassion: "Almost all the Maenads were unreasonable and many of them insupportable; it struck me in short that he [Aspern] was kinder, and more considerate than in his place (if I could imagine myself in any such place) I should have been" (156).

What the narrator seeks is the world of men without women, a world that he can get at only through the medium of pretended heterosexuality, where he must court Miss Tita in order to get at his true object of desire, the remnants of the artist he idolizes. The remnants are his "god" (155), and he will stoop to whatever is necessary to get at them. "Hypocrisy, duplicity are my only chance. I'm sorry for it, but for Jeffrey Aspern's sake I would do worse still" (159). The only thing he will not do—though he considers it for the briefest moment—is marry Miss Tita. The entrance into the bonds of matrimony carries a price too high even for his obsession. As Fred Kaplan rightly assesses, "Though the narrator is willing to lie, steal, perhaps even murder, to possess Aspern's papers, he recoils at and rejects the one sure strategy for obtaining what he covets. . . . He fears marriage more than he loves Aspern" (Kaplan, 319). If Miss Tita ever seriously thought the narrator would marry her, then certainly she was mistaken. "I hadn't given her cause—distinctly I hadn't. I had said to Mrs. Prest that I would make love to her [Miss Tita]; but it had been a joke without consequences and I had never said it to Tita Bordereau" (Aspern Papers, 246). His use of the word "victim" implies cognizance of his exploitation of Miss Tita and Miss Juliana. However, marriage is not and cannot be an alternative. The narrator of The Aspern Papers echoes the cry of the narrator in "The Figure in the Carpet," who says of marriage, "Oh that way madness lay."

As is characteristic of the fetish, the narrator's obsession employs bits and pieces of conventional romance for its erotic energy. Even though the narrator of *The Aspern Papers* has misogynistic tendencies, the letters he desires possibly refer to Aspern's love for women. Jeffrey Aspern was known to have had women worship him, and so represents to the narrator a sort of god of virility. He writes, "Half the women of his time, to speak liberally, had flung themselves at his head." The papers may also suggest heterosexual passion from their references to Miss Juliana, a woman of other than virginal repute: "There hovered about her name a perfume of reckless passion" (184). The narrator insists on describing his obsession in romantic terms and he transforms his "eccentric private errand" into a "general romance" (181), finding a parallel in his courting of the papers of Jeffrey Aspern with Romeo's courting of Juliet. "It was delicious—just such an air must have trembled with Romeo's vows when he stood among the thick flowers and raised his arms to his mistress's balcony" (187).

Another characteristic of the fetish is its guarantee of pleasure, whether by physically appropriating or by imagining the desired object. The narrator of *The Aspern Papers* describes the success or failure of his quest in physical terms, occasionally nearing orgasmic intensity. When he finds himself for the first time in the presence of Miss Juliana, his heart beats "as fast as if the miracle of resurrection had taken place for my benefit." Knowing that he is at last alone with her, he feels "a curious little tremor" from having come that much closer to the late Jeffrey Aspern (167). He feels an "irresistible desire" to make physical contact by holding hands with the woman who had known Aspern (172). He thinks of his satisfactions during the quest as some "great . . . gratification" (188). When he holds the photograph of Aspern, he hopes Juliana doesn't "perceive the tremor" of excitement in his clutch (216).

When the narrator discovers that he will never make physical contact with the papers, his despair takes the form of physical illness. He writes, "It made me quite sick to find myself confronted with that particular obstacle" (240). While Miss Tita's initially not burning the papers offers some "gratification" (241), when the papers finally do go up in smoke, the narrator blacks out. "The room seemed to go round me as she said this, and a real darkness for a moment descended on my eyes" (251). Despite a conclusion that denies fulfillment of the narrator's desire, the work still pays tribute to the sheer creativity and boundless energy of a man who finds some compensations outside the bounds of sexual convention.

Fetishism combines with other forms of sexual surprise in the short story "The Figure in the Carpet," which portrays a man kept from the deepest secrets of his literary profession because he refuses to marry. True, the reader has only the protagonist-narrator's word on that point, but his view is the view of his time. On several occasions, he laments the deprivations he must suffer from his failure to marry, for only marriage, so he thinks, can unlock the secret of his obsession, Hugh Vereker's work.

The text suggests this in part by the name of his competitor in the field of literary criticism, Lady Jane, a name borrowed from folk culture to connote heterosexual lust. Euphemisms for female and male genitalia, "Lady Jane" must have her "John Thomas." In James's story, the narrator must compete with Lady Jane for the attention of Hugh Vereker (the John Thomas of this tale). The narrator concedes reluctantly the powerful attraction between his competitor and their mutual object of desire, Hugh Vereker: "At three o'clock in the morning, not sleeping, remembering moreover how indispensable [Hugh Vereker] was to Lady Jane . . ." ("Figure in the Carpet," 370).

The narrator has his suspicions confirmed about the privileged intimacy between a man and a woman when two of his colleagues, Gwendolyn Erme and George Corvick, marry. Corvick, claiming to have found the secret to Hugh Vereker's work, refuses to share his findings with the narrator; however, the narrator suspects that Corvick does reveal his knowledge to his new wife. Only after marriage, which the narrator sees as removing the "last barrier to their intimacy," can one human being learn another's deepest secrets. So in marriage Corvick lets "the cat out of the bag" to Gwendolyn (391). After Corvick's death, the narrator supposes, mistakenly, that the secret about Vereker's work must also have passed on from Gwendolyn to her second husband, Drayton Deane. "The widow and wife would have broken by the rekindled hearth the silence that only a widow and wife might break" (396).

This cultlike fascination with the marriage vow as the fount of knowledge frustrates the narrator who is certain of one thing: he will never marry. Like the narrator in The Aspern Papers, this man will stoop to conquer only if the conquering requires no marriage vow. "Was the figure in the carpet traceable or describable only for husbands and wives—for lovers supremely united?" The narrator ponders this, and considers the possibility of marrying Gwendolyn. "Was I prepared to offer her this price for the blessing of her knowledge?" (391). His answer is that he is willing to pay any price *except* the ultimate price of matrimony.

Though the narrator is mistaken about Drayton Deane's knowledge of Vereker's work, his assumption is correct for society at large, where social success depends on marriage. If marriage is the key to success in society, what satisfactions remain for the bachelor? As in *The Aspern Papers*, the narrator in "The Figure in the Carpet" fetishizes another man's literary work. His obsession with Vereker's writings is fetishistic inasmuch as it distracts from the heterosexual aim detested by the narrator. In opposition to heterosexuality, the narrator's interests are partly homoerotic. The world of literature titillates him because it is inhabited almost exclusively by men (Lady Jane and Gwendolyn Erme are intruders), and he employs a vocabulary of sports, commonly associated with masculinity, to describe his literary profession. "Literature was a game of skill, and skill meant courage, and courage meant honour, and honour meant passion, meant life" (380). He believes that Vereker writes "as a man with some safe preserve for his sport." Vereker has after all assured the narrator that "a woman will never find out" the secrets of his work (372).

The homoerotic dimension of his obsession intensifies when the narrator meets Vereker in person and physically approaches the source of his fetish. He admits upon learning that Vereker has departed for good that the loss he will feel most poignantly is not that of any literary work. "I knew too which was the loss I most regretted. I had taken to the man still more than I had ever taken to the books" (378). In the presence of Vereker, the narrator takes pleasure in physical contact, when during their brief visit he takes Vereker's hand, and finds satisfaction when Vereker in turn touches him. "I can see him there still, on my rug, in the firelight and his spotted jacket, his fine clear face all bright with the desire to be tender to my youth." The narrator imagines that Vereker feels as he does: "I think the sight of my relief touched him, excited him."

The narrator also finds physical pleasure in Vereker's work. The language he uses to describe his search for the literary secret has a sadomasochistic edge. His experience with other critics is "as admirable when they patted me on the back as when they kicked me in the shins" (364). He notices Lady Jane "snatching" a place alongside Hugh Vereker, "brandishing" her criticism with "her longest arm." He appreciates the way Vereker "defeated" Lady Jane's purposes by "jerking" the paper out of her "clutch" (361). For the narrator, his profession proposes physical intensity, and because he perceives his profession as physical, a literary work can assume human dimensions and eventually overshadow, even replace, its author.[8] To describe a night of reading Vereker's work, the narrator says, "I sat up with Vereker half the night" (359).

The dimension of physicality introduces the element of autoeroticism as another form of sexual surprise. Other critics have detected this ability in the narrator of "The Figure in the Carpet" to arrive at stimulation without external physical contact; he achieves pleasure by distorting reality, describing his moment of greatest intensity in erotic terms. At the story's end, the narrator finds himself with Drayton Deane, who has recently married the widowed Gwendolyn Erme. Assuming that Deane must know the secret to Vereker's work because he has married the all-knowing widow, the narrator is shocked to learn that Deane knows nothing. His new spouse has told him "nothing about Hugh Vereker" (398). The narrator sadistically uses the moment he feels "quite to be my revenge" to inform the married man that his wife finds the strength to live only from her special knowledge concerning Vereker's work. In the next few minutes, the narrator feels an intimacy and sexual pleasure heretofore undocumented, rising and falling in a motion suggesting orgasm, from "original gleam" to "descent" to an "hour in the dark." As if to reflect his own pleasure, the narrator imagines that Deane utters "ejaculations" and feels a "shock" followed by a "throb" which then

> gather[s] into waves of wonder and curiosity—waves that promised, I could perfectly judge, to break in the end with the fury of my own highest tides. . . . I may say that today as victims of unappeased desire there isn't a pin to choose between us.

James's language suggests that the narrator's literary quest has been a sexual experience, which he recognizes as "almost my consolation" (400).[9]

Another alternative source of sexual pleasure appears in *The Portrait of a Lady*. Perhaps no other male character stands so obviously bereft of normal sexual pleasures as does Ralph Touchett, whose physical disability makes him avoid marriage, though he doesn't appear to resent bachelorhood. Like the marginal males mentioned above, Ralph Touchett finds pleasure elsewhere, in his case from what may best be termed voyeurism, as he enjoys watching the pleasure of others, in particular Isabel's romantic pursuits. He says to her, "I content myself with watching you—with the deepest interest" (*Portrait of a Lady*, 138). James depicts a man who at a young age has a diminished physical capacity, and who accordingly commits himself to a life of passivity, forbidding himself the "arts of demonstration" (38). The pleasure afforded Touchett may never brink that of sexual orgasm, but the pleasure he derives is nonetheless intense.

Indeed, orgasm is not considered "an essential part of . . . voyeurism"; the voyeur enjoys a more nebulous "erotic gratification" or "satisfaction" (Langevin, *Sexual Strands*, 381). The voyeur, or "scopophiliac," finds pleasure in viewing the gratification of another person, and is additionally gratified by a sense of power over the object of the gaze because the voyeur takes enjoyment from an unwilling and often unwitting partner, feasting as he does with the eyes (Langevin, 383). The partner may feel drained by the intensity of the voyeur's gaze, though he or she may gain if the ego is complimented by the gaze; however, if the gaze exceeds the boundaries of the partner's pleasure, the partner becomes victim rather than beneficiary, feeling trapped and powerless to incriminate the voyeur. Indeed, the pleasure of the voyeur is among the safest forms of sexual gratification for the perpetrator. "The stance of detached contemplation" provides "compensatory" eroticism that "relieves" the contemplator of "the burden of suffering that can come with more direct involvement" (Freedman, 193). It is difficult to convict someone for voyeurism or peeping because "there is no victim contact and the offender usually is not seen at all" (Langevin, 381-82). The object of the gaze can never attaint the voyeur except on grounds of suspicion. In this way the voyeur loses nothing.

These features of voyeurism surface in the way Ralph watches Isabel Archer. As the reader is told in *The Portrait of a Lady*, Ralph "lost nothing, in truth, by these wandering glances" (43). Ralph's gaze is fixed on Isabel: "He noticed everything that Isabel did" (131). On one occasion Isabel demands that Ralph leave her so she can be alone for a "simple and solitary repast." He pleads with her to let him remain, and she replies, "No, you will dine at your club" (135). The reader is then privileged to know Ralph's feelings at that moment: "It would have given him extreme pleasure to be present in person at the modest little feast she had sketched" (135).

He settles, however, for those few moments when he can be with her prior to her meal. His feelings here are characteristic of the voyeur, who learns to settle for whatever vista is offered him. The fuel of the voyeur's desire resides in a desire for satisfactions passively acquired with little or no risk. Ralph acknowledges at this moment precisely what his compensatory satisfactions are, and revels in them.

> For the moment, however, he liked immensely being alone with her, in the thickening dusk, in the centre of the multitudinous town; it made her seem to depend upon him and to be in his power. This power he could exert but vaguely; the best exercise of it was to accept her decisions submissively. There was almost an emotion in doing so. (135)

In Ralph's weighing of the situation, in his careful extraction of pleasure from what remains, his occupation as voyeur represents the paradigm of sexual surprise—maximum pleasure at minimum risk.

Most readers can only wonder at the compensations the voyeur finds. Ralph's father cannot understand, having lived a normal life as a functional heterosexual male. Daniel's is the aggressive life, having obtained wealth after having filled the preconditions of marriage and children, and so he naturally wishes that his son would follow in his footsteps, and in particular that he would marry. Ralph refuses and requests instead that half his fortune be given to Isabel. Deeply disturbed, Daniel tries to convince his son of the absurdity of his request, saying in reproach, "You speak as if it were for your entertainment" (171). Ralph admits, "I shall get just the good that I said just now I wished to put into Isabel's reach—that of having gratified my imagination" (172). (James describes Ralph as a man who seeks "his entertainment wherever he could find it" [233]).

Discovering Ralph's secret gratification, Isabel questions him. In defense, Ralph says, "Of course you mean that I am meddling in what doesn't concern me." Troubled by the sensitivity of the subject, he asks, "Why shouldn't I speak to you of this matter without annoying you or embarrassing myself?" (137). The law of the voyeur forbids verbalization; speaking about voyeurism robs the activity of its unique advantage of secrecy. Isabel's having found him out means a possible loss of his vantage point. "Ralph . . . had wished to see for himself; but while he was engaged in this pursuit he felt afresh what a

fool he had been to put the girl on her guard" (363). In lamenting his lost
advantage, Ralph reveals the intensity of his desire to see "all."

His passionate defense assures both Isabel and the reader that his voyeuristic activities are necessary to him. His pleasure is no game, but his very
raison d'être. He says to Isabel, "What is the use of adoring you without the
hope of a reward, if I can't have a few compensations? What is the use of
being ill and disabled, and restricted to mere spectatorship at the game of
life, if I really can't see the show when I have paid so much for my ticket?"
(137). Ralph brandishes emotional appeal with great skill as he tries to justify
behavior that to Isabel must seem ludicrous.

His need to see everything increases as Isabel removes herself from an easy
vantage point. After she is swept up by Osmond, Ralph's curiosity to see
intensifies, as does his awareness of his limitations as a marginal figure. What
concerns him is not so much living in the margins, but the viewing pleasure he
loses by not being more intimately involved. He thinks how Isabel "lived with
a certain magnificence, but you needed to be a member of her circle to perceive
it, for there was nothing to gape at, nothing to criticize, nothing even to admire,
in the daily proceedings of Mr. and Mrs. Osmond." He acknowledges that his
blind devotion to "seeing everything" has meant a disregard of human ties that
would have provided him with the riches of even closer observation. His passion
to see has become the center of his life: "What kept Ralph alive was simply the
fact that he had not yet seen enough of his cousin; he was not yet satisfied. . . .
Ralph had been kept alive by suspense" (365).

Voyeurism suits the marginal male, particularly as James interprets marginality. Fred Kaplan comments that the Henry James comfortably assumed
the role of voyeur as a child, inasmuch as he tended toward observation and
the powers of the imagination; from early on, James had a sense of himself
"as a voyeur, a keen observer of spaces, and thrusts, and relationships, of
being . . . dependent on his own eyes, feelings, memory" (Kaplan, 14). The
voyeuristic appeal persisted in James's travels to Europe, and in opposition
to William's self-assertion. Henry delighted instead in "reading, watching,
absorbing, without external interference or demands" (Kaplan, 28). Early in
life, James learned the pleasures that could be had from a voyeurism that
accommodated many of the sensations of active participation, but without
the responsibility—and without the punishment that might follow if actions
did not conform to conventional expectations.

In turn, James's fiction is a "poetics of seeing," depending on sight as a substitute for participation (Anderson, "Visiting Mind," 530). The marginal male thrives in James's fiction because he has accustomed himself early on to exactly the narrow space between activity and fantasy. His pleasure comes from what he sees that society does not see—the leftovers at the periphery of society's vision. By endowing the marginal male with voyeuristic qualities, James defines the essence of marginality: a fixated gaze on what the marginal male feels is forbidden him. In the process of gaping at what he thinks is forbidden, the man at the margins reaffirms his station by committing a forbidden act, namely voyeurism; fortunately for one such as Ralph Touchett, voyeurism is often impossible to detect. Finally, voyeurism transforms the marginal subject from the margins to the center of the reader's attention, for the voyeuristic gaze compels the reader to experience, if only for a moment, marginality in action. The reader is made an accomplice in the forbidden.

As typified in the aforementioned works, James's fiction frequently subverts traditional romance. Where the heterosexual plot fixates on courtship and marriage, James's tales "distract" the reader by focusing on "extracurricular" activities that seem to lead nowhere. The male gaze occasionally rests on the female but often strays to that "other" male sexuality. Perhaps no divergence from the norm is so distinct as homoeroticism, for which there is considerable evidence in James's fiction. *Roderick Hudson, The Princess Casamassima,* and *The Ambassadors* offer examples.

In *Roderick Hudson,* James explores homoeroticism through aesthetic appreciation of the male form. Rowland Mallet, the marginal male of this novel, finds in the young artist Roderick Hudson and his work all those masculine qualities that Rowland himself lacks. His admiration for Roderick reaches such a pitch that he must confess at Roderick's death "how exclusively, for two years, Roderick had filled his life" (*Roderick Hudson,* 387), that "there was no possible music in the universe so sweet as the sound of Roderick's voice" (383).

To some readers, it might appear that Rowland Mallet's main love interest is Mary Garland. True, he expresses a spiritual love for her, but as Roderick Hudson reminds his friend, Rowland's love for her lacks passion. Roderick distills his friend's interests in women when he says near the novel's conclusion, "Women for you [Rowland], by what I can make out, mean nothing. You have no imagination—no sensibility, nothing to be touched" (373). At least it seems so through the lens of heterosexuality.

Rowland's affections lie instead with the male, and his passion finds expression in his fondness for sculptures of male nudes. In the first half of the novel, James creates an artistic world of male nudes exclusive of female nudes. Rowland first encounters Roderick's male nude sculptures on a tour of the studio with Cecilia, who remarks, "If I refused last night to show you a pretty girl, I can at least show you a pretty boy" (59). Rowland sees in the first statue "a naked youth drinking from a gourd. The attitude was perfectly simple. The lad was squarely planted on his feet, with his legs a little apart; his back was slightly hollowed, his head thrown back; his hands were raised to support the rustic cup" (59). The text's attention to physical stance and youthful vigor attests to Rowland's keen eye for the male form.

As Rowland becomes better acquainted with Roderick, he comes to know other male figures shaped by his friend, including "a colossal head of a negro tossed back, defiant, with distended nostrils"; a young man resembling Roderick's long-lost brother; the figure of a lawyer; and a sepulchral monument of a young soldier "sleeping eternally with his hand on his sword" (72). These four figures appear prior to Rowland's introduction to Roderick's "Adam." Roderick is still searching for the woman on which to model "Eve," and so for the moment has his Adam living in an Edenic bliss sans woman.

The exclusively male statues are a metaphor for Rowland's fantasy, for he too wishes to live in a world without women. It is perhaps more than coincidence that the woman Roderick finds to model Eve after should be the woman who comes between himself and Rowland. In desperation Rowland says to Roderick, "There are two kinds of women—you ought to know by this time—the safe and the unsafe. Miss Light, if I am not mistaken, is one of the unsafe. A word to the wise!" (151). He says bluntly to Christina Light, "My feeling is this. Hudson, as I understand him, does not need, as an artist, the stimulus of strong emotion, of passion. He is better without it; he is emotional and passionate enough when he is left to himself. . . . I suggest most respectfully that you leave him alone" (231).

Christina threatens to invade Rowland's manly Eden, a world of resplendent, hard beauty. Rowland cherishes the hardness of Roderick's sculpted males, standing with their legs apart and their torsos thrown back in easy defiance of authority. This fascination with the solidity of the male nude sculpture reflects Rowland's appreciation for human males, for example, the figure of a "brown-breasted gondolier making superb muscular movements, in high relief" that both he and Hudson appreciate as they look out over the waterways of Venice. Rowland and Roderick together admire this young man in an aesthetic, Greek sense: "The only thing worth living for was to make a colossal bronze" of such a figure (107).

Rowland's fondness for the male form, founded in his aesthetic sense, sparks his fondness for the form of Roderick Hudson, who himself possesses that hard maleness. Rowland's passion for Roderick will be aesthetic to the end, when he gazes down at the corpse of his dead friend and examines it as he might a male nude sculpture whose face is "admirably handsome" (386), having already imagined Roderick in death long before the incident, "graceful and beautiful as he passed, plunging like a diver into a misty gulf. The gulf was destruction, annihilation, death" (251). Rowland's feelings suggest a wish to freeze Roderick's form in the permanence of stone.

His fondness for a physical hardness mingles with a fascination for emotional hardness. Here James explores a theme that will resurface in *The Princess Casamassima,* where one man loves the cruelty he sees in another. Rowland Mallet cannot help but fixate on the emotional hardness of his friend. He writes to Cecilia that Roderick "fascinates" him. "Yes, he *is* hard; there is no mistake about that. He's inflexible, he's brittle; and though he has plenty of spirit, plenty of soul, he hasn't what I call a heart" (238). Roderick has the uncanny ability (a feature of masculinity in Rowland's opinion) to display an utter lack of concern for other people, and this supreme selfishness both repels and fascinates Rowland. At the same moment that Rowland complains bitterly about Roderick's ignoring Mary's and his mother's pain at his absence, he admires Roderick's "extraordinary insensibility to the injurious effects of his eloquence": Roderick is "perfect," "clear-cut," "sharp-edged" (325).

Rowland envies in Roderick what he does not himself possess (75). At the Coliseum, Roderick's bravura astounds him, as he watches "Roderick clasp in his left arm the jagged corner of the vertical partition." Rowland feels certain the young man will drop to serious injury or even death, but thinks, "If the thing were possible he felt a sudden admiring glee at the thought of Roderick's doing it. . . . It would be finely done, it would be gallant, it would have a sort of masculine eloquence" (218). Rowland's adoration of Roderick is such that he mimics him in a later attempt to impress Mary Garland, all the while recalling the masculine superiority of his friend. It is perhaps this awe of Roderick's youth and vigor that lead him to treasure the times Roderick "passed his hand through Rowland's arm and they retraced their steps," when "Rowland felt his companion's arm trembling in his own" (71).

This adoration for the hard male who is both animal and machine appears again in *The Princess Casamassima*, where Hyacinth Robinson adores the revolutionary Paul Muniment. Like Rowland Mallet, Robinson represents the nonstereotypical male who never pursues women sexually but loves them spiritually. What he sees in men, however, is something other; his passion appears early in his acquaintance with Muniment. The two men are walking through London, when Hyacinth asks if he can be permitted to walk still further with his new companion. Muniment doubts Hyacinth's physical endurance, saying with a laugh, "I'll carry you, if you like." Hyacinth assures him, "I can walk as far as you." At this moment Hyacinth makes the connection of Paul Muniment's superior physical strength with political power. He feels a rush of admiration and "the desire to go with him till he dropped" (*Princess Casamassima*, 131). While this line foreshadows Hyacinth's end, when he literally "drops," it also reveals his wanting to lose himself in the superiority of Paul Muniment. Hyacinth says worshipfully to Muniment, "I would go by what you tell me, anywhere" (446).

Hyacinth is both repelled and fascinated by Muniment's ability to repress emotion. When Hyacinth tries to communicate to Muniment his concern over Hoffendahl's job, Muniment, at once tender and stone cold, responds, "You don't like it; you would rather throw it up" (442). Hyacinth thinks, "There was not in his voice the faintest note of irony or contempt. . . . Nevertheless the complete reasonableness of his tone itself cast a chill on his companion's spirit; it was like the touch of a hand at once very firm and very soft, but strangely cold" (442). Hyacinth, seeing in his friend the ability to show a little concern and then shut the doors of his emotion like stone, finds himself both the victim and "the passionate admirer" of Muniment's "hardness." Perhaps Hyacinth's admiration for this borderline cruelty comes in part from his own excess of sensitivity, though he has himself known the "perverse satisfaction . . . in turning the knife about in the wound inflicted" on others (218).

That Hyacinth adores Muniment is represented by the religious rhetoric used to describe their relationship, which finds a biblical corollary in the story of Jonathan and David alluded to in the final chapters of the novel when

Hyacinth is likened to the young David (583). What he feels for Muniment, described as "a purer feeling than love," echoes the sentiment between David and Jonathan. Other religious references include Hyacinth's dream of a "religion of friendship" where he can adore the man who "apparently cared nothing for women, talked of them rarely, and always decently, and had never had sign of a sweetheart" (205).

A surprising tenderness surfaces in their friendship when Muniment and Hyacinth walk on the slopes of Greenwich Park. Stopping to rest, Hyacinth gazes into Muniment's face. "For a minute the two men's eyes met with extreme clearness" (441). Hyacinth thinks of "the sweetness of loafing there" on the hill (443). His fondness for Muniment is such that he can be moved to tears at the thought of betrayal (393), and then again he can feel "vile" with jealousy (535).

The mingled pain and pleasure of homoeroticism surfaces in *The Ambassadors* in Strether's combined revulsion and admiration for the urbane Chad Newsome, the man of supreme masculine ease. The homoeroticism of this novel takes the form of what Leon Edel calls "cautious hedonism" (Edel, 5:71), with a character steeped in the sexual timidity that one critic calls "virginal" (Davis, *Sexuality and Textuality*, 5). Strether has married, but far from initiating him into the world of sexual pleasure, his marriage seems to have stifled eroticism. Like the bachelor Rowland Mallet in *Roderick Hudson*, Strether shows "timidity toward sensuality" (Davis, *Sexuality and Textuality*, 6).

His life before Europe must have convinced him to adopt a certain narrowness that allows pleasure only in marriage and family, if at all. As is typical of the sexually shy, Strether possesses that "virginal passivity" that translates into "ignorance in the terms of sexual knowledge" (Davis, *Sexuality and Textuality*, 142). Europe introduces him to sexual possibilities that he can hardly deny, as in the theater with Maria Gostrey, where he acknowledges the enormous "personal and sexual range" of Europeans. Strether at first feels guilty; his experience in Europe might "demoralize" him (*Ambassadors*, 37). Even were he not to act against Mrs. Newsome's wishes, he still feels tainted by forbidden pleasures that the puritanical Waymarsh blames on the Catholic Church. Strether thinks, "These first walks in Europe were in fact a kind of finely lurid intimation of what one might find at the end."

In Strether's mind, no other individual illustrates the sexual energy of Europe so completely as does Chad Newsome. Strether discovers in Chad a hardness similar to what Hyacinth Robinson found in Paul Muniment. Chad is "thick and strong" (99), "sleek" (184) and "hard" (141). No title fits Chad more appropriately than that of "pagan," conveying in a word all the rugged-ness and sexual vitality that stands at a pole opposite the life Strether has known until now. Strether envies Chad, finding himself inferior in sexual prowess. He experiences the homoerotic admiration that a man feels when he would like to be another and cannot be so, and yet derives enormous pleasure from that admiration. Strether's comment to Bilham is tinged with both envy and a certain attraction (what James calls the "stirred sense"). Strether says to Bilham, "I know—if we talk of that—whom I should enjoy being like!" (133).

What Strether sees in Chad is his ease with women, that trademark of ideal masculinity in a heterosexual society. Chad is "the young man marked out by women" (98), possessing the urbanity and masculine ease to function with women in a way that mystifies Strether, who finds emotional compan-ionship with women rather than sexual pleasure. Chad's hardness allows him to consider leaving Madame de Vionnet after she has invested enormous emotional energy in a relationship with him, a man who is considerably younger than she is, at a point in her life when she has few years to find new romance. Strether meanwhile is horrified that Chad could consider leaving, and expresses his horror to Madame de Vionnet in saying, "You're afraid for your life!" (322).

At the same time that Chad horrifies him, Strether adores the "palpable presence" of "massive young manhood" that gives off the undeniable hint of "some sense of power, oddly perverted" (99). Chad's perverse power is the power to live the pleasures of Paris and then return to Woollett unscathed. For Strether, the road of pleasure is always one of expenses, exacted in the form of guilt and verbal retribution from the likes of Mrs. Newsome and Waymarsh. Chad rises up as the male who operates cleanly, with maximum pleasure and minimum waste.

The admiration that Strether has for Chad, homoerotic in clinical terms, symbolizes the gap between those males who benefit by the status quo, and those, like Strether, who are disenfranchised. The marginal male in Henry James's fiction looks outward and sees what he would like to be, and then turns inward and interprets as a lack the difference he finds there. The gap between reality and wishes is the locus of desire, a source of both pain and pleasure, and the space in which the marginal male will live out his private moments. With this quotient of pain and pleasure, James weaves the unique tale of men who creatively seek gratification of sexual desire. What society finds distracting, the man at the margins finds interesting; their margin becomes his center.

The very presence of such marginal characters calls into question the established code. Though James does not promote revolution, content as he is to find livable spaces in the established order, still the life he gives to these characters is testament to the failure of the status quo to accommodate dissonance and a testament to the struggle of marginal characters to find personal satisfaction in a society that almost invariably punishes deviance.

4

Language

Henry James staked his reputation on his linguistic abilities, a fact exemplified by his sudden panic when, after moving to England, he could not at first muster the high level of conversation he had grown accustomed to in America: "I am losing my standard," he wrote, "my charming little standard of wit, of grace, of good manners, of vivacity, of urbanity, of intelligence, of what makes an easy and natural style of intercourse" (quoted in Edel, 227). James knew, on a seemingly visceral level, the extent to which speech defines a person. A profound knowledge of language could improve one's station, while substandard usage could cripple a person for life.

One might assume therefore that mastery of language for James meant the ability to clearly communicate information. Do not people who have mastered the language of a particular community "say what they mean"? On the contrary, James's language moves beyond the informative function to become instead a medium rich in evocation. Indeed, at the height of his abilities, James appears to have resisted the informative function of language to the point of confusion. One could say that he *transgressed* common assumptions about the reasons people speak and write.[1]

James's transgression of the bounds of ordinary speech is to some extent an inherent feature of literary language, in the "business of . . . deception" (Cross, *Contingencies*, 5). While ordinary speech struggles to inform its audience about the world "out there," literary language consciously creates its own reality, depending not so much on a preexisting condition, but rather on the illusion of such dependency. According to Pierre Macheray, the plot of a novel strives in the opposite direction from ordinary speech: where ordinary speech has as its paradigm the efficient, even speedy, relaying of facts, the successful literary work "progresses only by the inhibition of truth; its movement is an ambivalence, an effort to postpone rather than to hasten revelation" (Macheray, *Theory*, 29).

While James's style participates in a delayed manner common to literary language, his style also moves beyond this convention to a conscious, even excessive elaboration that brings direct communication to a near standstill. James experimented with a writing style sufficiently indirect to drive many readers to outright anger. As has been mentioned in an earlier chapter, his brother William is perhaps the most famous example of a reader more than disgruntled by James's increasingly labyrinthine style, despising Henry's tendency in *The American Scene* to "avoid naming it straight," and instead "breathing and sighing all around it." William begged his brother to "say a thing in one sentence as straight and explicit as it can be made, and then drop it forever. . . . Say it *out*, for God's sake, and have done with it!" (quoted in Edel, 5:301).

William James's condemnation cannot be easily dismissed, for his complaint addresses the essence of James's style, particularly of the later works, whose sentences wind seemingly endlessly around the subject, burying thematic keys within an almost impenetrable text. In *The Ambassadors*, a work replete with Jamesian difficulty, James uses the technique of indirect language to describe Chad Newsome. (The indirect style reflects Chad's customary reticence). In this passage, Lambert Strether is admiring Chad, but the text refuses to surrender the precise motive for his admiration. Instead the text tosses up vague passages such as "Chad himself was more than ever"; Chad is "in Miss Barrace's great sense, wonderful"; and Chad impresses Strether "as knowing how to enter a box" (127).

In another passage, Strether is again admiring Chad, but this time the reader must guess the object of Strether's gaze. He is looking across the garden at Gloriani and the Duchess when "there was something in the great world covertly tigerish, which came to him across the lawn and in the charming air as a waft from the jungle." The sentence that follows seems to refer back to the Duchess and Gloriani with the phrase "the two"; however, the text implicitly pairs Gloriani and Chad. Strether then says he would wish to resemble one more than the other. Bilham responds much as the reader might, asking if Strether refers to Gloriani. Only in the following paragraph is the reader supplied with the information necessary to guess the true object of Strether's gaze, Chad Newsome. Yet even this passage never explicitly confirms Chad as the admired one, but relies on the reader's prior knowledge of Strether's fondness for the young man. The text suggests a wealth of information, yet confirms nothing: the subject of the passage has been plunged beneath a gilt textual surface, refusing easy surrender.[2] James never speaks "the informing word" (127), or if he does, it is delayed and concealed in a dense text.

In later years, even James's private letters began to assume this indirect style, exemplified in his correspondence with Hendrik C. Andersen. Where his audience sought facts, he plunged them beneath a decorated surface, supplying information to only the most sensitive reader. Where James's letters to Andersen might have nakedly exposed his condemnation of the young man's "megalomania," James denied his audience any outright condemnation. In a letter dated August 10th, 1904, James finds fault with the "scale" of Andersen's art yet conceals his dislike under an extended metaphor of the "blazing comet." While James admits being terrified by the artwork, through linguistic indirection he softens the blow by transforming his horror at Andersen's art into a deep concern for the young man's safety:

> [The art work] is magnificent—it is sublime, it is heroic; and the idea and composition . . . evidently a very big thing. Only I feel as if it were let loose into space like a blazing comet—with you, personally, dangling after like the tail, and I ask myself where my poor dear confident reckless Hendrik is being whirled through the dark future, where he is going to be dropped. I want to be there, wherever it is, to catch you in my arms. (*Letters*, IV, 310)

James could have written directly, "Your art is offensive to me, and is a harm to you." Instead, he concealed his condemnation to the point of extinction, trusting that the careful reader (namely, Andersen) will detect and heed his subtle message.

Examined in terms of surrender or denial, James denies the reader the anticipated, unadorned response.[3] Where he might be powerless in other areas, in the field of language James wielded enormous power. His unique writing style takes on the dimensions of a political act, inasmuch as "political" can mean any action that empowers the individual in relation to the larger community; in the manner defined by Julia Kristeva, James's discourse challenges "the law of language" and so becomes a form of "social and political protest" (Kristeva, *Desire*, 65). He refuses to "supply the focused image" that society depends on to reveal dissension from the norm; his art is "subversive because it undermines clarity" (Boren, *Eurydice*, 12, 15). Obedience to social expectation through the use of normative prose concretizes the status quo, insofar as direct language exposes and ultimately punishes its speaker.

James's labyrinthine style, on the other hand, circumvents any attempt at silence and annihilation at the hands of the authorities, whoever they might be. The indirect style of his "later work had as its motivation a desire to elude censorship" (Boren, 23). As Walter Anderson suggests, James employed "enigmatic language" to avoid the public exposure that would reveal the shocking nature of what he was saying (Anderson, "Visiting Mind," 527).

Jonathan Freedman contends that James tended ever toward the aestheticism heralded by his competitor and sometime enemy, Oscar Wilde, insofar as aestheticism celebrated the intrinsic value of art, visual stimulation, detachment, and even eroticism, which James himself ascribed to. With some modifications, according to Freedman, James borrowed from aestheticism the "self-indulgence" and decadence at odds with social conventions. His mode of handling aestheticism, however, differed from Wilde's in the "supple maneuverings of Jamesian prose" that suppress, evade, or efface dangerous elements that might be censored. His style of self-censorship allowed for the existence of questionable elements that express themselves indirectly by silence, qualification, allusion, and implication (Freedman, *Professions*, 135-136). His enigmatic language so successfully shrouds the revolutionary content of his prose that the evidence the censor seeks is as elusive as Hugh Vereker's figure in the carpet.

The height of James's indirection is the favoring of image over concept. As Boren argues, James later style becomes "increasingly metaphorical [and thereby] obscure" (Boren, 38). Metaphor obscures meaning by emphasizing beauty over truth, producing a language that offers "compelling images rather than definite concepts" (Macheray, 56). In the majority of the above-mentioned examples of James's writing, his language revolves around images that obscure and nearly consume any concepts surrounding them. Whether he uses the metaphor of a man "entering a box," or the "glossy, male tiger," or a "blazing comet," the images are striking enough to propel themselves by their own energy, apart from any ideas they may represent. "Indeed at their most characteristic, James's metaphors provoke a feeling of arbitrariness and extravagance, a sense of an uncomfortable break in the organic connection of things, that can be deeply disturbing" (Yeazell, *Language*, 40).

Round about and in and out, James's language follows a labyrinthine trail not unlike the indirect style he attributed to Honoré de Balzac in his Harvard lecture "The Lesson of Balzac." Of the French writer he said,

> From the moment our imagination plays at all, of course, and from the moment we try to catch and preserve the pictures it [Balzac's writing] throws off, from that moment we too, in our comparatively feeble way, live vicariously—succeed in opening a series of dusky passages in which, with a more or less childlike ingenuity, we can romp to and fro. ("Lesson," 84)

James's mention of "dusky passages" and an "opening" suggest a freedom from traditional usage constraints, liberating Balzac from censorship. James continues, "Balzac's luxury . . . was in the extraordinary number and length of his radiating and ramifying corridors. . . . The relations of the parts to each other are at moments multiplied almost to madness" ("Lesson," 85).

Like Balzac, James tried to elude the cultural expectation of clarity. Is this intentional "transgression" of language malicious? Does James "misuse" language to abuse his audience? Perhaps, though from another perspective his style saves the reader from a kind of emotional tyranny that pervades normative prose, insofar as normative language pretends to speak "the truth." T. S. Eliot noted in James's writing "his mastery over, his baffling escape from[,] ideas" (Zabel, "Introduction," 28). James's stylistic development increasingly questioned the ability of language to convey the "truth" about anything whatsoever. A false claim to "truth" perhaps touched a nerve in the writer who despised tyranny in all its forms. His secretary Theodora Bosanquet wrote of James's intense desire "not to exercise any tyrannical power over other people"; his "Utopia was an anarchy where nobody would be responsible for any other human being but only for his own civilized character" (quoted in Zabel, 29). Writing with indirection, James could give the reader ample room to agree or disagree with his ideas.

Any time people are empowered by language, they assume the burden of deciding how to use that power. While no linguistically empowered person is ever relieved of the risk of abusing others with language, the person who best resists tyrannical tendencies is one who attempts to use language only to enhance personal freedom and, whenever possible, the freedom of others. To do otherwise would be to erode the personal freedom of others, where one person's freedom is conditional on another's imprisonment.

Linguistic tyranny is apparent in the short story "The Pupil," first published in 1891. In this tale, a young man, Pemberton, is hired to tutor the son of Mr. and Mrs. Moreen, who survive by good appearances. The Moreens use language in the form of coded speech known as "Ultramoreen" to safeguard their sham existence. Their language allows them to exploit the good intentions of the marginal Pemberton and promotes an atmosphere of neglect that demoralizes and ultimately destroys the other marginal male in the story, their young son Morgan.[4]

The Moreen household appears to be the social ideal of the nuclear family. On the surface, Mr. and Mrs. Moreen have healthy children who are exquisitely provided for, materially and culturally, in the climate of Europe's jet set. However, this ideal family is all form and no substance. Beneath the sham, the Moreens live on the edge of survival. The source of their income is unknown, and what money they have is not enough to maintain genuine prosperity. James implies by the Moreens' close-knit appearance the sham of social convention that buys surface respectability at the cost of happiness.

The Moreens maintain their shabby existence with words. The language spoken in the Moreen family is a bizarre dialect invented by the parents, different from standard usage in its technique of indirection similar to that used by James, though perhaps less dependent on metaphor than upon other forms of obfuscation. By means of abstractions, vagueness, and hyperbole, the Moreens rhetorically conceal the falseness of their position.

When Pemberton first enters the Moreen household, he is thrown off balance by their abnormal speech; the Moreens' manipulation of English alienates him from a language he thought he had long ago mastered. Instances of difficulty in the language used by the Moreen family are numerous. Mrs. Moreen favors vagueness in her speech. She says to Pemberton early in his career as tutor, "Oh, I can assure you that all that will be quite regular" ("Pupil," 219). Pemberton wonders what "all that" means. He thinks of Mrs. Moreen's language as inclusive of both "vagueness and point," both here and everywhere, where he can only guess at the meaning. When Mrs. Moreen says to him concerning Morgan, "He's a genius—you'll love him!" (221), the word "genius" rests heavy on his mind. "Genius" is ambiguous, for it depends on the context in which it is spoken. As Mrs. Moreen uses the term, she might mean any one of a number of things. She might be saying that Morgan possesses a daunting intellect that precludes likability; if that is what she means, then she speaks sarcastically when she says, "You'll love him!" On the other hand, she might intend to say that Morgan is indeed likable because he understands things, because he's intelligent. The ambiguity prevents Pemberton from analyzing the situation accurately.

This indirect speech ultimately traps Pemberton in an undesirable situation where is he forced to tutor his charge without adequate remuneration. Just when Pemberton thinks he has escaped the Moreen household, he is informed by telegraph that his former student Morgan is ill. Out of love for the boy, he reluctantly returns, only to be trapped by Mrs. Moreen's words. She makes Pemberton's thoughts of escape unconscionable: "She continued to talk and surge vaguely about the little draped stuffy salon while Pemberton sat with the boy, whose colour gradually came back; and she mixed up her reasons, hinting that there were going to be changes" (260). The vague swirl of "changes" and "reasons" keeps Pemberton in the dark and overwhelms him with guilt sufficient to force him back into servitude.

Besides the use of vague rhetoric, Mrs. Moreen also employs hyperbole to imprison Pemberton. Her web of exaggeration, bordering on outright lies, makes Pemberton her "inmate" (240), as she begs him to make a "sacrifice" (240), suggesting to Pemberton that his service to them has assumed the grand proportions of some holy ritual that would weigh heavily on Pemberton's conscience if not carried out in full. Her hyperbolic references to sin, guilt, and death persist when she says to Pemberton, "You put the knife to my throat." Her language transforms Pemberton's assignment into a weighty battle of life and death that he cannot, in good conscience, abandon. The young man's imprisonment in Mrs. Moreen's words illustrates the structuralist concept of language, which portrays language as inherently community-based, robbing the individual of autonomy. As Frederick Jameson has argued, language can indeed function as a "prison house"; words have their "own independent life, and will not stoop to the beck and call of individual intentions" (Eagleton, Literary Theory, 112). So it is that Pemberton's entrance into the world of Ultramoreen presupposes his unwitting loss of freedom at the hands of his more articulate captors.

Meanwhile, the young boy Morgan also suffers from his parent's abuse of their linguistic powers. Though male and potentially the inheritor of the family power, Morgan seems more the victim of that language than its beneficiary, unable as he is to use it to his own ends. His manhood brought as it is into question by his poor health and emotional sensitivity to his parents' charade—which he cannot interpret as anything but false—he is haunted literally to death. Morgan is swept by the force of language into a world that he cannot endure, dragged into a world deadened by a language that fails to speak for him, losing all identity except for the one imposed upon him by his parents.

To highlight the power of language to manipulate and even destroy a life, James describes Morgan's life as a text; he has been written onto the page of life and can as easily be erased. Pemberton reads the text of Morgan's life and sudden death as some "phantasmagoric" novel, a "mystic volume in which the boy had been amateurishly bound" (223). Lacan says of the power of language to imprison the individual,

> Symbols in fact envelop the life of man in a network so total that they join together, before he comes into the world, those who are going to engender him 'by flesh and blood': so total that they bring to his birth, along with the gifts of the stars, if not with the gifts of the fairies, the shape of his destiny. . . . The word absolves his being or condemns it. (Lacan, Ecrits, 68)

The language of Ultramoreen creates Morgan and then kills him. Pemberton must sit and watch, powerless to save the boy because he himself is victim rather than beneficiary of that language.

Pemberton's closeness to Morgan prior to the young boy's death is due in part to the way the boy's language differs slightly from that of his parents. In the course of their friendship, only Morgan seems willing to invite Pemberton into the otherwise closed family circle. After all, as marginal players, Pemberton and Morgan have much in common. Though trained in

Ultramoreen, Morgan speaks to Pemberton in a more direct fashion, describing the baseness of his parents' sham. Stripped of artifice, Morgan's language threatens to expose the paucity of the Moreens' existence: "Morgan made the facts so vivid and droll, and at the same time so bald and so ugly" (248). However, being endowed with a language that hides the terrifying reality of their existence, Mr. and Mrs. Moreen remain unscathed. These wielders of linguistic power shape their world as they will through a language they have altered to suit their purposes.

The story "The Pupil" is perhaps James's most explicit treatment of language, particularly in terms of empowered speakers and their less articulate victims. That James should select marginal males—Pemberton and Morgan—as the victims of linguistic tyranny is more than a coincidence, for these are examples of a character type predisposed to such social disadvantage. An already precarious relation to the status quo is further threatened by the marginal male's misapprehension of language: characters like Pemberton operate under the illusion that following the conventions of language as they have been taught as a child will one day secure for them a place in society. Offended by intentional manipulation of language, Pemberton is unable to "misuse" language toward his own ends.

This misplaced confidence in correct speech comes in part from an assumption that language "correctly" used can best communicate what the speaker means. However, the assumption that language can so communicate is just that—an assumption, in Lacanian terminology "bad faith." Literary theorists have in the past several decades introduced a concept of which James appears to have been prescient: that the written or spoken word "lacks" the ability to accurately name anything. The denotative function of language is fundamentally flawed because, according to Lacan, a word can only replace the subject in the attempt to name it: "The symbol [the word] manifests itself first of all as the murder of the thing" (Lacan, 104). Existing independently from both the world the individual imagines he sees and the world as it really is, the symbolic world of language can only approximate the "real," in so doing creating its own reality. In Lacan's way of thinking, to believe in the ability of language to say anything accurately is akin to worshipping a false idol, as language insists on betraying its followers.[5]

To add to this inherent lack, language is at best a borrowed tool. Mrs. Moreen's manipulation of Pemberton epitomizes the linguistic concept that language is the key to the individual's entrance into a particular culture and also the snare to which the speaker inevitably sacrifices a portion of the self. Language is constantly reshaped by the culture that speaks it, and more often than not serves to reinforce the dominant cultural myth, disavowing ideologies at its margins and so disempowering marginal individuals. According to Roland Barthes, language that blindly serves the culture forces a "tyranny of meaning" upon the recipient (quoted in Eagleton, 135), with a tendency to naturalize the dominant ideology of society, to "convert culture into nature." In normative language, the speaker transmits cultural notions with no thought that his language transmits only one view of reality. Ordinary speech—direct rather than circuitous, unadorned rather than adorned—is "quite neutral and colorless in itself: it's only job is to represent something else, become the vehicle of a meaning conceived quite independently of itself. It must interfere with [the ideology] it mediates as little as possible" (Eagleton, 136). According to Barthes, language of this sort assumes an unassailable rightness, robbing the marginal individual of any unique voice.

If one adheres to Barthes's and Lacan's line, since language tends toward tyranny, then it must be willfully altered by the individual speaker into something personally useful. Empowered speakers recognize that they operate in a linguistic mine field where traps are set by the culture to secure the cultural norm. Language assumes physical dimension as speakers recognize language for what it is, a tool for potential empowerment that is often wielded by society as a weapon of conformity. Barthes advocates nonnormative usage that calls into question the power structure. Speakers of nonnormative language conscientiously battle with the mode of the day by forcing language to account for itself, and so betray cultural assumptions. For Barthes, a "healthy" use language avoids "determinate meaning," or "settled signifieds," and is instead "plural and diffuse, an inexhaustible tissue or galaxy of signifiers, a seamless weave of codes and fragments of codes" (quoted in Eagleton, 138), that empowers the individual speaker against the otherwise engulfing shadow of the dominant culture.

Language thus employed reflects and validates the marginal speaker; language and speaker support each other in an identity apart from normalcy. In 1917, Rebecca West complained that James's circumlocutions were no longer "the straight young thing that could run where it liked," but now "a delicate creature swathed in relative clauses as an individual in shawls"

(West, *Henry James*, 41). Her gendered words take on special meaning for a man caught in the androgynous middle of bachelorhood, unverified by masculine pursuits and unexpressed in normative prose. By allowing the "marginal aspects of syntax—the conjunctions, prepositions, modifying phrases and dependent clauses—to carry crucial significance and govern its structure," James forces the text off-center (Cross, *Contingencies*, 29). This avoidance of clarity through linguistic distractions stylistically advocates the author's marginality.

James's prescience on this point is demonstrated in *The Portrait of a Lady*. The difference between the marginal male Ralph Touchett in this novel and Pemberton in "The Pupil" in terms of the marginal figure's use of language is that while Pemberton resists the "full repertoire" of language after a forced introduction by the Moreens, Touchett willfully plays with language in what Barthes describes as a spirit of *jouissance*. Pemberton submits to the linguistic tyranny of others, while Ralph plans his own word games. From the contrasts between these two characters, Pemberton and Touchett, the reader may observe the necessity of becoming an active rather than a passive player in order to appropriate the power of language.

Ralph Touchett customarily conceals himself behind a form of indirect speech not unlike that used by the Moreens. Significantly, he uses this speech arguably in the service of individual freedom, as opposed to the tyranny exercised by the Moreens. After acquainting herself with Ralph's odd speaking style, Henrietta Stackpole can only wish that Ralph would be more direct. Her wish corresponds with that of other "custodians" of culture who zealously serve cultural norms. In a rare instance of directness that delights Henrietta, Ralph discloses his affections for Isabel. Henrietta responds, "That's the most natural speech I have ever heard you make" (*Portrait of a Lady*, 114). Such "natural speech" signals a surrender of power because what Ralph discloses to Henrietta becomes her domain, and because Ralph's direct language doesn't say at all what he means. Once uttered, his words are nonretractable; Henrietta will "take him at his word." For her, language associated with the subject of romantic love invariably speaks truths that the speaker himself may not be privy to. Like the analyst who finds the analysand unwittingly condemning himself, Henrietta Stackpole traps people by their language. She is the person Ralph must forever hide from, for she squeezes from the spoken word every particle of meaning to satisfy her world view,

leaving the speaker bereft of individuality. Ralph must now create an elaborate scheme "to prove to you [Henrietta] that you are wrong" (114).

This is not the only occasion when Ralph must be on guard against what
are for him ill-suited social expectations. Like Henrietta Stackpole, Ralph's
father acts as a social custodian. Daniel Touchett rarely speaks, but when he
does, Ralph listens respectfully, automatically assuming the role of the dutiful
son; the scenario is set then for Ralph's powerlessness. During one of Ralph's
visits to his invalid father, Daniel says, "Who is that with me—is it my son?"
Ralph responds in a manner that reinforces the father-son dynamic: "Yes, it's
your son, daddy" (165).

Clear from the outset is the subject of the conversation, marriage, which
Ralph tries desperately to steer away from. His father says, "I want to talk
about you"; Ralph says, "You had better select a brighter topic" (166). Daniel
nevertheless forges ahead with the distasteful topic of marriage. Ralph
incorrectly assumes that his father speaks of marriage because he has renewed
confidence in his son's recovery from illness, at which time Ralph will truly
be an eligible bachelor. However, Daniel does not believe that Ralph's health
will improve *before* marriage, but rather that his life (and presumably his
health) will improve only *after* marrying. In Daniel's view, Ralph must marry
as soon as possible, in the throes of illness if necessary; the perpetuation of
a bachelor's existence would be unhealthy, unnatural, even sinful.

Daniel's style of speaking is direct, the kind of "natural speech" Henrietta
Stackpole is fond of, as she says to Ralph, "All you want is to lead a natural
life. It is a great deal more natural to marry a pretty young lady you are in
love with than it is to remain single on false principles" (169). Daniel
Touchett's prosaic utterance implies absolute confidence that what he says
will convey with precision what he means. If language is itself a custodian of
the dominant culture, then Daniel's confidence in using terms like "natural"
and "false" suggests that he supports the status quo. He need not define his
terms since, in the patriarchal world he inhabits, his ideas are assumed to be
correct. His abstract vocabulary is not intentionally vague (different from the
intended abstraction of Ultramoreen in "The Pupil"); rather, his words are
meant to convey with precision his disapproval of his son's not marrying.
The father warns his son that a life carried out on such false principles will
surely be a "sin." The abstract notion of "sin," were it not so deeply rooted in
the cultural context of heterosexual culture, would otherwise need further

definition. As it is, he can say with assurance, "I don't think I enter into your spirit. It seems to me immoral" (171).

Ralph launches a linguistic counterattack against his father. He knows that his father will consider him "immoral" for toying with life by choosing to give his money to Isabel rather than financing her through marriage, an action repugnant to the financially shrewd Daniel. Yet it is this same "immoral spirit" applied to language that helps Ralph evade the clutches of his father's argument. The "immoral spirit" (play versus seriousness) occurs in Ralph's use of metaphor where he toys with the language in a way that unsettles his father momentarily. He employs a metaphor of a ship to represent his relation to Isabel: "I should like to put a little wind in her sails" (169). The metaphor momentarily confuses his father, rhetorically allowing Ralph the space to then define himself in a more direct fashion: "I should like to put money in her purse." Now Daniel finds himself forced to operate in terms of Ralph's metaphor, for only a metaphorical response could accommodate the implications of Ralph's words. When Daniel disagrees through metaphor, then Ralph extends the metaphor: "I should like to see her going before the breeze" (171). The pleasant metaphor of ship and sails evokes the happy sensations Ralph will gain from witnessing the experience, not to mention the sizable financial gain for Isabel. Ralph has gained the upper hand in the argument, as he says to Daniel, "It's scandalous, the way I have taken advantage of you" (172). Though Daniel refuses to "enter into" Ralph's "spirit," nonetheless he can't respond adequately to Ralph's metaphors. As Linda Boren has said of the situation, "A question posed by [The Portrait of a Lady] is how to live imaginatively in a world circumscribed by language" (Boren, 44). Ralph attempts to do just that by exceeding the bounds of his father's prescriptive prose with the creative use of metaphor. His behavior exemplifies Ruth Bernard Yeazell's observation that the "elaboration of . . . metaphor becomes an assertion of control over a potentially threatening experience," a way of talking oneself into authority (Yeazell, Language, 44).

Julia Kristeva explores the ways that language can move beyond the "normal" to the "poetic" (or "literary" to use Macheray's terminology) in the fashion illustrated by the confrontation of father and son in The Portrait of a Lady, employing the term "semiotic disposition" to categorize various modes of speech. Ralph's "semiotic disposition" employs poetic language, defined as "the over-determination of a lexeme by multiple meanings" (Kristeva,

Reader, 28): his metaphors elicit an array of associations to unsettle his father's complacent rhetoric. Daniel's symbolic disposition on the other hand favors denotation over connotation, and information over evocation; he trusts that "he means what he says," assisting society as he does in the formation of "that reassuring image which every society offers itself" (Kristeva, *Reader*, 31). He uses a "logical, simple, positive and 'scientific' form of communication, that is stripped of all stylistic, rhythmic and 'poetic' ambiguities," a form of speech "logically assumed by the role of the father" (Kristeva, *Reader*, 151).

Meanwhile Ralph employs language for its evocative rather than its informative function, the "capacity for enjoyment," in the "transgression" of intended meaning (Kristeva, *Reader*, 29), exemplifying the speaker who is conscious of the power of language to renew "the order in which he is inescapably caught up" (29). His use of poetic language illustrates Kristeva's theory that language creatively employed can indeed disrupt the boundaries set by society. While ordinary speech proclaims deceptively to know and understand reality, and thereby promotes certain ideologies, a language that emphasizes image over concept admits the lack of any language to ever fully name reality, and thereby *"reveals* the gaps in ideology" (Macheray, 60).

That James should himself have used an indirect style, and moreover have encouraged indirect usage by his marginal males, suggests his linguistic awareness of concepts akin to Kristeva's semiotic disposition. He seems to have been aware of and keenly interested in two opposing types of discourse, one that favors established codes and another that subverts the status quo by means of language manipulation. James's most complete study of language associated with the marginal male appears in the novel *The Ambassadors*. Like Pemberton in "The Pupil," Lambert Strether early on assumes that proper use of the language will guarantee him the keys to the world; if he knows the symbols well enough, he will achieve power. However, his experience forces him to test the limits of language, moving from his faith in direct communication to his manipulation of language through indirection, and finally to the farthest remove from normative speech, his use of silence.

Strether bases his reputation on language. The numerous conversations between Strether and Maria Gostrey, with whom he so often "filled up the time" (325), represent the most polished verbal communication in the novel. James creates in Strether a character who attracts the reader's sympathy largely because he is skilled in conversation. His manner of talking associates him with the generous and good-natured. Indeed, psychological studies of this persona employ adjectives like "easygoing," "enthusiastic," "cheerful," "participating," and "warm-hearted" (Crown, "Psychological Correlates," 38, 39). One could ascribe any number of these qualities to Strether, who thinks of "pleasantness" as one of his greatest assets (*Ambassadors*, 209).

His conversational manner and the accompanying implied surrender of self are further demonstrated in the way he judges other people on the basis of conversationality. He repeatedly applies adjectives connoting warmth and well-being to people who have mastered easy, intimate verbal exchange. Madame de Vionnet is one such person. Strether imagines that her eyes "moved in and out of their talk, back to the quarter of the warm spring air, in which early summer had already begun to throb, and then back again to his face and their human question" (176). On one occasion, after recalling that Madame de Vionnet "had told him things," Strether feels as if he has been dipped in water, not "chill" but of a "pleasant warmth" (155). "She was not a wandering alien, keeping back more than she gave, but one of the familiar, the intimate, the fortunate" (172).

Strether associates less conversational characters with coldness, perhaps the coldest figure being Mrs. Newsome, whom he describes simply as "cold" (195). Jim Pocock agrees, likening Mrs. Newsome's and Sarah's silences to the behavior of fierce animals who wear their "warm side in" (215). Exposing cold faces to the world, mother and daughter are fiercest when they are silent; Jim says, "It's at feeding-time that they're quietest" (216). Maria confirms Strether's opinion of Mrs. Newsome when she defines her adversary as "all cold thought" (296).

Strether proudly assumes the "burden" of speech in the service of others, hoping to gain something for himself (though he will claim otherwise) in the end, wearing his language like a badge of service: "No one could explain better when needful" (92). He accepts the burden even when the task appears Sisyphian: Strether "held that nothing ever was in fact—for any one else— explained" (92). While he vaguely perceives the failure of his speech, his clinging to language suggests that he hasn't internalized the limits of language. His greatest aim would be to sweep the *sky* clear for lucidity; however, if he can't do that, he is content simply to keep "the *ground* free of the wild weed of delusion" (emphasis added, 92). He shows a dim awareness of the futility of language, but frantically fills every gap as if that limitation never existed, because silence terrifies him.

So he accepts the burden of Mrs. Newsome's assignment, and in so doing revitalizes his sense of self-worth. Explaining the affairs of Paris to Mrs. Newsome "was a practice that continued, oddly enough, to relieve him, to make him come nearer than anything else to the consciousness of doing something" (194). Defined by his verbal skills, and now fulfilling that definition, he promises to explain to Mrs. Newsome nothing short of "everything" (153).

The gap is wide, however, between what Strether thinks language is doing for him and its actual effect. Other characters exploit Strether's easy, conversant manner to achieve their ends; he is their slave because he is a slave to language. To recall the theories of Lacan, Barthes, and Kristeva, language tends to serve the community rather than the individual. Strether's "bad faith" in the linguistic norm intensifies his marginality.

The gap widens between belief and reality if one looks at language as inseparable from the institution of heterosexuality. The language Strether speaks inherently serves the heterosexual code; his words contradict his intentions by all the while promoting moral and sexual expectations of the majority. According to Lacan, the conveying of meaning through prescribed language is itself a metaphor for the continuation of patriarchy from one generation to the next. This cradle-to-grave "enthrallment" of language marries the individual to the culture which that language represents (DuPlessis, *Writing Beyond*, 2). A marginal character such as Lambert Strether, unable to fill the expectations of the society whose language he speaks, is a believer without the promise of sanctification.

Fortunately for Strether, from the moment he sets foot in Europe, his "bad faith" in language begins to crumble. In England, he finds himself in a world quite other from the puritanically ordered one he has known in Woollett, discovering here a threatening ambiguity where things are seldom what they appear. He encounters a European usage that intends indirection, whereas he has been accustomed to direct speech. His initial response is to call this intentional vagueness "immoral" and "evil." Maria Gostrey says to him, "You feel as if this were wrong," referring to Strether's guilt-ridden enjoyment of the hours before the arrival of Waymarsh, who represents to Strether all the puritanical restraint of New England. At her words, Strether cries, "Then get me out!" (*Ambassadors*, 26). The reader is privy to the prevailing "evil" when Strether goes to the play with Maria. There, introduced to the world of drama that lives and breathes the artificial medium, Strether discovers that the world of the stage has come off the proscenium and into the audience, transforming the world of real people into "types" as seemingly unreal as those in art. Maria Gostrey has already appropriated this knowledge, and says offhandedly concerning the people in the audience, "Oh yes, they're types." This world is composed of metaphor, a world described not in prosaic language, which presumably the world of Woollett has come to depend upon. Strether thinks, "It was an evening, it was a world of types, and this was a connexion above all in which the figures and faces in the stalls were interchangeable with those on the stage" (43).

Strether considers language a vehicle for the unreality around him. Rather than attempting to describe objects with precision, his neighbors in the theater attest to the impossibility of such a task and even celebrate that indirection. The "great stripped handsome red-haired lady" next to him talks in "stray dissyllables" composed of "so much sound that he wondered they hadn't more sense." The light and sound describe not details, but the "very flush of English life" (44).

The vagueness of light and sound also confuses the roles people play. Whereas Strether previously attempted precision in a prosaic fashion, as if to reflect the rigidity of male and female roles, in England he discovers enormous "personal and . . . sexual range" (44), where things, because they are not rigidly defined, can be simply as they are. With the ecstasy of the alchemist, Strether plays with the shifting element "as, before a glass case on a table, it might have passed from medal to medal and from copper to gold." Woollett's prosaic reality gives way to the European model of poetic possibility.

In Paris, Strether confronts the full potential of indirect speech. Arriving in Europe armed only with "Woollett words" that a "more subtle culture" exposes as inadequate (Cross, 41), Strether feeds voraciously on "short gusts of speculation—sudden flights of fancy in Louvre galleries, hungry gazes through clear plates" (Ambassadors, 63). The substance of this overwhelming display is a circumvention of the carefully channeled communications Strether has been accustomed to in Woollett. Where Puritanism ruled in New England, now this ambassador finds his freedom both exciting and threatening. In the vagueness of the light and sound of Paris he finds, disconcertingly, shades of meaning he cannot decipher.

His greatest uneasiness seemed to peep at him out of the imminent impression that almost any acceptance of Paris might give one's authority away. It hung before him this morning, the vast bright Babylon, like some huge iridescent object, a jewel brilliant and hard, in which parts were not to be discriminated nor difference comfortably marked. It twinkled and trembled and melted together, and what seemed all surface one moment seemed all depth the next. (65)

Strether cautiously considers the power of this communication that operates outside the linguistic rule he is accustomed to.

Kristeva would perhaps call the New England prose to which Strether is accustomed "direct," "object-oriented," "monological," or "realistic," terms that each in their own way point to a language employed for its informative value, little given to *jouissance*. What Strether confronts in Europe violates his definition of language as information. The language of his Parisian friends challenges "official" linguistic codes and laws in the manner described by Kristeva; this new language is "ambivalent," "connotative," "double" (Kristeva, *Reader*, 36, 43).

Strether at first struggles against this new language by maintaining the prosaic style of Woollett, which ultimately fails him. When speaking to Chad Newsome, Strether's words fall on ears deaf to the power of authority, for Chad has circumvented that authority with the linguistic freedom of the Continent. Strether says to him in halting, unadorned prose, "I've come, you know, to make you break with everything, neither more nor less, and take you straight home; so you'll be so good as immediately and favourably to consider it" (94). In the context of indirect speech in which Strether's statement appears, his directness may shock the reader; its baldness contrasts with the beauty of the poetic language that surrounds it. Chad receives Strether's words with grace, but Strether ends up defending what he has said, rather than Chad justifying his actions in Paris.

This experience shocks Strether, who intended to fulfill his duty to Mrs. Newsome without delay, and he considers, "What it came to was that with an absolutely *new* quantity to deal with one simply couldn't know" (95). The conflict rests on a simple failure of the traditional channels of communication; Strether's customary usage failed to meet the challenge of the situation. "The new quantity was represented by the fact that Chad had been made over." Strether's dated notions of language must therefore be revised: "He had originally thought of lines and tunes as things to be taken, but these possibilities had now quite melted away. There was no computing at all what the young man before him would think or feel or say on any subject whatever" (96).

Strether's "bad faith" in the linguistic norm promulgated by Woollett deteriorates further after a conversation with his friend Bilham, whom he depends on to apprise him of the relationship between Madame de Vionnet and Chad. Bilham looks Strether "full in the face" and tells him, "It's a virtuous attachment" (112). The seeming clarity of Bilham's speech refreshes Strether to the point of giving him "almost a new lease on life" (114). He is momentarily seduced by the "truth" of Bilham's words, much pleased by what Lacan calls "empty speech," as distinguished from "full speech." Empty speech reinforces the status quo, similar to the "determinate speech" used by Ralph Touchett's father in *The Portrait of a Lady*. Just as determinate speech gives society a positive image of itself, so empty speech performs a similar function for the individual who bathes in the afterglow of a language that always reaffirms a cherished self-image, however false that image may be. On the other hand, "full speech" disturbs false assumptions. Bilham's words are empty speech to Strether, who wishes desperately to believe that Chad and Madame de Vionnet have indeed remained "virtuous" in their "attachment." Only after much evidence to the contrary does he reluctantly realize that Bilham has lied to him (117). Having acknowledged falsehood, Strether's "bad faith" in normative language disintegrates further. He has all the while depended on other speakers to be direct and now he finds that his "morality" of usage has little application. He feels victimized by a more complex language that relies on indirection to suggest, rather than give, information.

Shortly thereafter, Strether receives an invitation to Gloriani's garden, a place that overwhelms him with its various mediums of communication. The garden echoes with myriad sounds, each carrying some vague message in a place that "had the sense of names in the air, of ghosts at the windows, of signs and tokens, a whole range of expression, all about [Strether], too thick for prompt discrimination" (120). The place lends itself to the "aesthetic lyre" (85). In the conversations of the guests at the garden party, poetry supplants prose and the literal turns metaphoric. Strether can hardly begin to absorb the exquisite yet vague conversation between Miss Barrace and Bilham, in both of whose words he senses a world of illusion where things are not what they seem but instead adopt the loudest plumage for enhanced effect. Miss Barrace creates so much beauty out of nothing that Strether can but stand back and admire her as the observer who views everything "as before some full shop-window" (125). In a few minutes, Barrace and Bilham's conversation includes the metaphors of cannibals, Christians, bones, biblical prophets, and Indian chiefs. This visual potpourri runs counter to the strong sense of "reality" Strether has always assumed should be expressed in language. He asks Miss Barrace whether things in Paris are ever shown as "they really are." She replies, "Oh I like your Boston 'reallys'!" (126). His concern over their apparent detachment from reality peaks when his two companions describe Waymarsh in outrageous metaphors. Bilham says that Waymarsh is a Moses "on the ceiling, brought down to the floor; overwhelming, colossal, but somehow portable" (125). Miss Barrace calls Waymarsh an Indian chief who "stands wrapt in his blanket and gives no sign" (126). Barrace and Bilham's metaphors communicate in exciting mental pictures a surprising truthfulness. Their metaphors "assert a kind of witty verbal control over the entire . . . situation, even while they call heightened attention to it" (Yeazell, *Language*, 53).

The visual quality of this language fascinates Strether even as it offends him. In Strether's mind, "reality" has for his companions found a substitute in obscenity, notwithstanding the concealed truth in what they say. Strether wonders if this linguistic game might be immoral.[6] "You've all of you here so much visual sense that you've somehow all 'run' to it. There are moments when it strikes one that you haven't any [moral sense]" (126). Miss Barrace answers that it is the "fault of the light of Paris." People and things are not themselves, but likenesses. "How can it be helped? We're all looking at each other—and in the light of Paris one sees what things resemble" (126).

Like Ralph Touchett in *The Portrait of a Lady*, Strether begins to realize the power of indirect language to circumvent the prosaic authority of the day. Like James's own circuitous style, the language of Paris refuses "to supply the focused image" (Boren, 12). Strether's acceptance and participation in this alternative community delivers a resounding no to the demands of Mrs. Newsome and Waymarsh, who speak in a language that borrows from established channels of authority.

However, James does not stop with the exploration of indirect speech; he also introduces the effectiveness of the absence of speech. The possibility of silence as a means of communication is introduced during Strether's correspondence with Mrs. Newsome. He has been commissioned to communicate Chad's activities in Paris but is troubled by how to convey the positive change in Chad. He considers writing the words, "Have at last seen [Chad], but oh dear!" While this exclamation would communicate to Mrs. Newsome the disastrous consequences of Chad's Paris life, it would in no way encompass his strong attraction to this new Chad, whom he likens to a lustrous "tiger" (133). Then again he considers writing, "Awfully old—grey hair" (93). This locution again would fail to convey what he means, that is, his innocence when compared with Chad's experience. Strether wishes that *"she* [Mrs. Newsome] would come out" to discover things for herself (104).

Mrs. Newsome never visits Europe, remaining remarkably distant, with the ever-widening gaps between her responses to Strether's letters creating an ominous silence that tests Strether's dependency on verbal expression. Because his strategic position between two worlds, coupled with his communicative skills, might be expected to enhance his significance for others, Strether is shocked when Mrs. Newsome writes less frequently as tensions mount. Indeed her somewhat acid responses have dwindled to nothing. "He was now clearly following a process by which Mrs. Newsome's letters could but logically stop" (195).

Despite its apparent ineffectiveness, Strether's obsession with verbal communication persists. He increases his writing in proportion to the decreases in Mrs. Newsome's correspondence; the silence created by Mrs. Newsome must somehow be filled. "He might have written before more freely, but he had never written more copiously." The justification he gives for his actions seems superficial: "He frankly gave for a reason at Woollett that he wished to fill the void created there by Sarah's departure" (195). Strether fears the unspoken and unexplained, and he must at least attempt articulation of "the facts." He tends to see Mrs. Newsome's silence as not valuable in itself, but "a deficiency to be overcome, . . . not the explanation . . . but the negation of explanation" (Dauenhauer, *Silence,* 87-88). Strether momentarily misses much of the significance behind Mrs. Newsome's silence.

In his frantic attempt to fill the silence, Strether begins to realize that Mrs. Newsome's silences are powerful: "It struck him really that he had never so lived with her as during this period of her silence" (195). In his attempt to say everything, has he become obsolete, a figure "whistling in the dark, . . .

beating the sense out of words?" (194). Meanwhile, the "ghost of the lady of Woollett" strengthens her hold on him, in her silence and her absence "more importunate" for him than "any other presence" (195).

Strether also confronts the silences of his old friend Waymarsh. Their meeting in Europe ends years of separation; they had not "during years before this meeting in Europe, found so much as a day for a meeting" (30). It might be expected that the two friends would talk freely in an effort to compensate for the years of silence, but surprisingly, Waymarsh leaves much unsaid, amounting in Strether's view to "the element of stricken silence" (30). Like Mrs. Newsome, Waymarsh confronts Strether with silence, leaving him to grope for the right words. Strether tries to humor his friend, but his attempts at conversation are both futile and pathetic. On one occasion Strether initiates the conversation by saying, "I've all sorts of things to tell you." He "put it in a way that was a virtual hint to Waymarsh to help him enjoy the telling" (71). Rather than responding with warmth, Waymarsh is silent, causing the verbose Strether to call out "Merçi, François!" when the waiter brings the meal, all in an attempt to break the silence. During this period of silence, Strether alleviates his distinct discomfort by sipping from his wine glass, wiping his mustache, and contemplating two nearby English women.

Waymarsh's silences are "the tool of conquest and the invincible adversary" (Auchard, *Silences in James,* 157); the silences that Strether calls "sacred rages" terrify him. After enduring them for some time, Strether escapes to the French countryside, where he can live without "fear of his [Waymarsh's] company," reminiscing about how "he had been most of all afraid of Waymarsh, in whose presence, so far as they had mixed together in the light of the town, he had never without somehow paying for it" attempted to speak French (303). Waymarsh's silent criticism is effective because it leaves Strether to "formulate the charge," preventing him from any defense: "It was . . . as if he missed the chance to explain his motive" (*Ambassadors,* 199).

Waymarsh's silences become more significant when Strether learns of his friend's clandestine communication with Mrs. Newsome. It seems to Strether, shortly before Waymarsh leaves France, that his companion's mood is lighter. What has happened is that Waymarsh has written to Mrs. Newsome. Strether "had a quick blurred view of daily cables, questions, answers, signals," the result of Waymarsh's "forcing his fine old natural voice" (272). Waymarsh's silence, then, has been directed exclusively at Strether. Mrs. Newsome's and

Waymarsh's silence secures them a position of power over their verbose friend.

Another instance of silence even more explicitly reveals to Strether its value. He goes to Sarah Pocock's apartment to await the "sound of the oracle [Sarah]" (247), but in place of Sarah's "sound," he enters a silent apartment occupied only by Mamie, who stands gazing out the window, unaware that anyone has entered the room. Strether appreciates as never before this surprise moment of silence, to him "a point not to have been reckoned beforehand." While normally he would have met the silence with words, this time "the oddity was that when he *had* watched and considered he simply stepped back into the room without following up his advantage." His moment of silence allows him to meditate on the advantages he might gain from developing his friendship with Mamie: his sense of remarkable women felt "ready, this afternoon, . . . to include her" (248). The possibility of a relationship is awakened in the silence that words would normally have filled, a relationship that proves useful to Strether, for in the conversation that follows the silence, Mamie promises to confront Sarah in defense of Strether.

Some chapters later, a crisis ensues that revolves around significant silences. While Strether assumes his normal verbosity, other characters employ silence to their own practical advantage. Strolling through the French countryside, Strether sees two figures in a boat off in the distance. Upon discovering these figures to be Madame de Vionnet and Chad, he gesticulates wildly, seeking visual, and of course verbal, communication with his friends, "agitating his hat and his stick and loudly calling out—a demonstration that brought him relief as soon as he had seen it answered" (308). Extensive verbal communication continues after Chad and Madame de Vionnet come ashore, and Madame de Vionnet launches into an explanation in a difficult French that Strether can hardly comprehend. Even more noticeable, however is Chad's near silence. The two people who owe an explanation hardly speak at all, leaving Strether to fill up the silence. Once again, Strether comes to the rescue; he "was to reflect later on and in private that it was mainly *he* who had explained" (309).

Strether has fallen prey to his two friends' uses of silence. Not limiting themselves to verbal communication, Madame de Vionnet and Chad had apparently employed a convenient moment of silence to prepare for their confrontation with Strether: "Their only conference could have been the brief instants in the boat before they confessed to recognizing the spectator on the bank, for they hadn't been alone together a moment since and must have communicated in silence." Strether is obviously struck by such a phenomenon. "It was a part of the deep impression for Strether . . . that they *could* so communicate" (312). And what was communicated is precisely that Madame de Vionnet would provide the explanations while Chad remained silent: Chad would "leave it to her," it seems to Strether. At one point in the conversation, Chad silently leaves Madame de Vionnet to justify her being out late without proper dress, placing the blame not on them both, but on *her* "imprudence."

Oddly enough Strether does not condemn Chad for this behavior. What he notices in Chad's silence is power. Strether thinks, "There had been as yet no such vivid illustration of [Chad's] famous knowing how to live" (312). Chad's taciturn manner leaves him both free of implication and supremely significant. For all Strether's verbal exercises, it is for Chad that Madame de Vionnet performs that evening, and it is Chad whom she wishes to protect by not returning to their intended lodgings later that night (312).

For all his conversational skill, Strether is insignificant in Madame de Vionnet's life. It is painful for him to hear Madame de Vionnet some time later say that she and Chad would like Strether to be as he always has been, a pleasant conversationalist. She expects him to visit them at their whim, to live "not 'with' us, if you object to that, but near enough to us, somewhere, for us to see you—well, . . . when we *must* " (321). Strether feels abandoned because she has, however politely, defined the difference—and distance— between himself and the romantic pair. When Madame de Vionnet tells him at the end of this conversation that she has always wanted him, he retorts that she has already "had" him (324).

The concern for Strether is how to achieve significance as Chad and others have. He decides to meets his needs as he has observed other people filling theirs, through silence. His silence occurs in a conversation with Maria just before he leaves Paris. She explains to him that Madame de Vionnet wants Strether to forgive her adulterous relationship with Chad. Upon discovering that Strether does not judge his friend harshly, Maria asks him if she should communicate his true feelings to Madame de Vionnet. His response is emphatic: "No. Tell her nothing." By committing Maria to silence, his significance for Madame de Vionnet will be infinitely enhanced, because she will never discover that he has forgiven her but will instead suffer in his silence.

To read for significant silences in *The Ambassadors* enhances what James has called a "drama of discrimination" (*Ambassadors*, 7). That Strether gains something at the novel's end is widely acknowledged, contrary to the statement he makes to Maria that he has "Not, out of the whole affair, . . . got anything" for himself. In fact, he may gain more than many readers have thought, for Strether empowers himself through the same practical application of silence that allows other characters like Chad Newsome to achieve their own, even selfish, ends.

Strether's turning to silence shows James at perhaps his most modern, as he attempts to see language in a new way. In depicting a temporary abandonment of language, James penetrates an essential paradox of literary usage: his turning to silence in *The Ambassadors* suggests the *necessary* function of silence in any profound exploration of language, inasmuch as language depends on what is *not* said. As Macheray contends, "In order to say anything, there are other things *which must not be said*" (85). What does a person's utterance conceal? What might have been said in its place? And in literature, why is this story told and not another?

A discussion of silence is a discussion of the margins. Acceptable speech implies a judgment about what should be kept silent, just as ways of life considered acceptable imply the existence of unacceptable lifestyles. In James's exploration of silence as employed by the marginal male, he fuses the margins of language and life. That Strether should turn to silence means that he turns to a domain that, on a symbolic level, should be familiar to him. It could be said that silence suits Strether because much of his existence depends on silence; to say too much about his life would mean censorship of the very things that give him pleasure. His acquaintance with silence as a source of power means his conscious willingness to embrace the unsaid, just as unconsciously his survival has all along depended on the unsaid. If language tends to trap one in cultural biases, then silence is the most complete renunciation of these traps in favor of the individual. Silence as an attitude "challenges the assumptions of our civilization" (Hassan, *Literature*, 15).

In Strether's use of silence, however, the reader may note a word of caution. The capable speaker who moves beyond language to silence runs the risk of being silenced right out of existence. While an excessive dependency on normative prose renders the marginal subject captive to the culture, absence of language in the form of prolonged silence threatens the subject with erasure. Either extreme could lead to a psychological crisis. James leaves the reader with just enough uncertainty at the end of *The Ambassadors* to raise the question of whether Strether has gone too far in severing communicative ties. He has no future in Paris, and his future in Woollett seems questionable without enormous effort on his part to create new relationships through language.

Language is necessary for identity: It is impossible "to live in sanity in an archaic, preverbal state"; voice is "essential to being" (Boren, 83, 85). Though language ultimately fails to name the object of discourse, at least it provides a starting point for interaction with the culture. Silence is fine to explore on occasion, but its depths promise destruction, as James demonstrated in an earlier novel, *The Princess Casamassima*.[7] Upon his return to Woollett, only through language can Strether begin to shape anew the relationships that make a social being. Strether says in the end, "I shall see what I can make of it" (344). Having realized the deadening quality of language, he can proceed to an empowering use of language as he remains conscious always of its limits.

5

Absent Fathers

Henry James knew all too well the peculiar effects of a father's absence on a son; a father can haunt a son in his absence as if he were physically near him. James's fiction in part explores what he had discovered in life—how marginal sons exploit the freedom of an absent patriarchy only to discover that the patriarchy is all-powerful even when absent.

The influence of the absent or "dead" father has long been a favorite subject of psychologists. Freud contributed the notion, based on his readings of William Robertson Smith and others, of the father as the creator of society. In *Totem and Taboo*, a work less accepted now as accurate in itself than as a precedent for later study, Freud draws up a framework of the primal father who must be murdered by his sons because of his boundless authority.[1] The father insists both that the son be like him and that he not be like him, for the father can do at least one thing the son cannot—have intercourse with the mother. That is the father's "prerogative" (Freud, *Reader*, 642).

As suspect as some details of Freud's theory of the primal father may seem to many readers today, the idea of the father as more powerful in death than he ever was in life has proven relevant in the modern age. According to Freud's theory, the father's literal presence diminished his power because the son resented his tedious influence. Freud explained the primal father's *enhanced* power after death, as the sons elevate him to totemic status and worship the laws he bestowed upon them to relieve their guilt at having murdered him. After the "death of the Father,"

> a sense of guilt made its appearance, which in this instance coincided with the remorse felt by the whole group. The dead father became stronger than the living one had been . . . What had up to then been prevented by [the father's] actual existence was thenceforward prohibited by the sons themselves. (Freud, 501)

Such continued obedience to the laws of the father allayed in part the original guilt over murdering the father; society must symbolically honor the dead father in order to conceal a communal crime.

Jacques Lacan extended Freud's observations about the death of the father in order to examine the effects of the patriarchy, or symbolic fathers. According to Lacan, the dead father can be evoked by the mere mention of his name: "The image of the Punisher scarcely needs to be brandished for the child to form it. Its effects are more far-reaching than any act of brutality" (Lacan, Ecrits, 11). Lacan's Name-of-the-Father is a term that encompasses fathers of all types, evoking "all . . . higher authority" encountered by the son (Eagleton, Literary Theory, 156). He equates the Name-of-the-Father (or symbolic father) with Law. Society is arranged so as to elevate the Father and the Law so they become worthy of the child's complete obedience and obeisance.

However, promises of satisfaction for the child are illusory; since the child wants nothing more than to return to the state of imagined bliss with the mother, any promises for satisfaction made by the fathers—familial and extrafamilial—are, according to Lacan, a hoax. The Law and the Father pretend to be the bearers of superlative satisfactions, while what the son really wants is something the Father cannot give:

> Whether in fact he is one of those fathers who make the laws or whether he poses as the pillar of the faith, as a paragon of integrity and devotion, as virtuous or as a virtuoso, by serving a work of salvation, of whatever object or lack of object, of nation or of birth, safeguard or salubrity, of legacy or legality, of the pure or of impure, all ideals that provide him with all too many opportunities of being in a posture of undeserving, inadequacy, even of fraud. (Lacan, 219)

Fathers, both literal and symbolic, promise what they can never give and so stand as impostors before the child.

For James, the power wielded by the absent father held great significance because of his relationship with his father, Henry James, Sr. However, to trace this pattern, it is necessary to go back two generations: Henry James, Sr., had known the effects of a tyrannical patriarch from his father, William James of Albany, who had measured his son's activities by a draconian book of ethics. Henry Senior imaged his father as a "stern and uncompromising parent," "virtually a god" (Edel, *Henry James*, 4:22). The pressure of paternal authority and the guilt at defying that authority became so great that, according to Leon Edel, it precipitated in Henry Senior a psychological breakdown. "The inner terror of defying Fathers and escaping spectral eyes was finally too much for him" (Edel, 4:31).

The oddity is that William of Albany should ever have been perceived as a tyrant. Accounts reveal that Henry Senior's father was rarely in the household. "He was usually out all day, appearing only for the evening meal, where, at the head of the table, he must have made an imposing, if often a silent, figure" (Lewis, *Jameses*, 17). Apparently William of Albany worked an effect on his children in his absence, becoming more powerful the less he remained in the household. Henry Senior was subject to this influence when he went away to school: "The felt presence of his father's power and influence was not restricted to Albany; it pervaded the very atmosphere of the college in which Henry was enrolled" (Lewis, 21).

To avoid becoming a tyrant himself, Henry Senior took the road of leniency, encouraging in his own household a laxity bordering on chaos, believing that his children should live "free and uncommitted." This laxity was countered by his wife's forceful but inconsistent discipline, such that their son Henry Junior would observe later in life, "We wholesomely breathed inconsistency and drank contradictions" (Edel, 4:7).

The memory the novelist came away with above all was that of a father amputated both physically and emotionally—an absence of sorts. Henry Senior's early loss of a leg foreshadowed later emotional crises which left him, in the wake of his own father's excessive paternal authority, ineffectual as a parent. To his sons, he often appeared the buffoon. The younger Henry said of his father, "Our dear parent could have told us very little, in all probability, under whatever pressure, what had become of anything" (Edel 4:51). James's

dissatisfaction with his father participates in a common discontent of nineteenth-century American authors toward ineffectual fathers. As Quentin Anderson observes, "It is a striking fact that our nineteenth-century literature was
conditioned by the failure of the fathers, and that their sons did not accept
them as successful in filling the role popularly assigned them" (Anderson,
Imperial Self, 11).[2]

It might seem that Henry Senior's absence would mean a lack of influence
on the younger Henry. However, just as the absent William of Albany had
nonetheless held power over his son, so Henry Senior would leave his mark on
the younger Henry. His was what William Veeder has termed a lethal weakness,
pervading his son's life with considerable force. While on the one hand he
advocated freedom, he wished people to define their freedom on his terms. He
admitted, "My disposition is so tyrannous that I can hardly allow another to be
comfortable save in my own way" (quoted in Kaplan, *Henry James,* 16). One
example is Henry Senior's odd combination of religious freedom and fervor. On
the one hand, he exhorted his sons to follow their inner religious impulses while,
on the other, he overwhelmed them with what Howard Feinstein calls the
"immobilizing web" of religious passion (Feinstein, *Singular Life,* 302).

In addition, his insistence on his sons' liberal education meant that while
Henry and William could pick and choose from the ideologies of teachers
at nine different schools and four different countries, socially they were
thrown back to a dependence on the family; their travels in Europe "cut them
off" from lasting extrafamilial friendships. "Stimulating, privileged, yet erratic
and unpredictable, the James family subtly undermined independence"
(Feinstein, 302).

One influence particularly hard for the younger Henry to shake was his
name, as he was his father's namesake. While naming might seem insignificant to the outsider, to James it meant four decades of struggle for his own
identity: for the first forty years of his life Henry James signed his name with
"Jr." to distinguish himself from his father. Only upon the death of his father,
in 1882, would he finally feel independent enough of the father to drop the
appellation, a rejection which might be viewed through the Lacanian lens of
rejection of the Law: to refuse a name (or in James's case a part of name) "is
to refuse the Father as Lawgiver" (Nelson, "Familial Isotopy," 134).

While the literal father, Henry James, Sr., played a surprisingly significant
role in James's life by means of absence, the Name-of-the-Father (the

symbolic father) was also important. Who served as a symbolic father in James's life? In other words, by whom would James come to define himself, and to whom would he feel the need to answer? These questions lead inevitably to Henry's older brother, William. Throughout his life, William was his younger brother's sharpest critic, the one Henry felt bound to answer to. Indeed, Henry James saw his older brother as forever outdoing him. He wrote that his brother "had gained such an advantage of me in his sixteen months' experience of the world before mine began that I never for all the tie of childhood and youth in the least caught up with him or overtook him" (quoted in Edel, 4:59). William was to his younger brother "superior and radiant," the "renewedly dazzling brother" who both early and late laid down "the law" in the brothers' affairs (quoted in Lewis, 237).

William criticized his younger brother's social life for being "superficial," devoted to a large number of people at the expense of "a deeper one at a few points" (Lewis, 316). This appears to be at least a concealed disapproval of Henry's bachelorhood and his resistance to any one romantic attachment. William early on also judged his younger brother's attempts at fiction harshly, accusing Henry of "losing touch with American speech" (Lewis, 548). When Henry compiled his travelogue after his return to America in 1904, the elder brother accused him of shallowness. Even concerning works of Henry's maturity, such as *The Golden Bowl*, William played the role of the "perceptive" critic without "being altogether appreciative" (Lewis, 189). When both brothers were nominated for membership in the National Institute of Arts and Letters, William rejected the offer, saying somewhat superciliously, "I am the more encouraged to this course by the fact that my younger and shallower and vainer brother is already in the academy (quoted in Kaplan, 518). At William's death, in a combination of sorrow and acuity, Henry wrote, "From far back in dimmest childhood he had been my ideal Elder Brother, and I still, through all the years, saw in him, even as a small timorous boy yet, my protector, my backer, my authority, and my pride" (quoted in Lewis, 584).

Henry James was haunted even in his brother's absence, answering to his older brother when William was thousands of miles away, separated from Henry just as Lambert Strether is separated from Mrs. Newsome by the wide gulf of the Atlantic Ocean. The brothers shared a "curiously intimate although geographically removed relationship" (Myers, *William James*, 22), maintained by "a massive transatlantic correspondence" (Kaplan 392), and maintaining as well a psychological link that spanned the Atlantic; often they felt ill at the same time or sensed the other's illness, rendering sickness an expression of "psychological connectedness" (Feinstein, 303). Henry on occasion spoke of his brother's recovery from illness as a cure "for us" both (*Notes of a Son and a Brother*, 444). When Henry was in extreme ill health just before his death, his nephew Harry reported that his uncle "seems often to think that my father [William] is here, *tho' not in the same room*" (quoted in Edel, 4:59). Thus, years after William's death, Henry was still haunted by his brother.

The geographical distance that Henry maintained between himself and William represented his desperate attempt to combat all patriarchal influences, particularly that of his brother; Europe provided in James's fiction and in his life a partially successful escape from the strictures of Puritan America. Drawing an analogy between James's experience and that of *The Ambassador's* Lambert Strether, Leon Edel comments, "[James] had long before decided that his choice of Europe was wise, that Woollett and Mrs. Newsome—that is, the U.S.A.—could not offer him the sense of freedom he had won for himself abroad" (Edel, 5:69-70). Europe offered to the American expatriate a supreme freedom, and James felt that America needed to lose itself in some European tradition; America needed an ancient past, for it had too long cherished a paucity of beliefs to the point of obsession. In Europe, meanwhile, the American male could wander at ease sexually, theologically, philosophically, and, above all, aesthetically. His senses could be gratified, often and without punishment.[3]

James here reveals a paradox, for on the one hand he belonged to the "gentry elite" of America and knew from birth the privileges that accompany such membership. To belong to this elite sector meant to bear witness to some tenable claim to high culture that uniformly critiqued what was crude, ugly, and basely material in American society. Then again, James shared the prejudice held by the American elite that America lacked any culture measurable against that of Europe (Freedman, *Professions*, 129). To be American and gentrified was to endure the sometimes unpleasant combination of prestige and mild humiliation. James responded by returning to Europe to claim any cultural inheritance left to him.

He adored Europe from the time he was a young man, associating the Old World with all things cultural and sensual, reporting on the "promiscuous

London life, . . . a wonderful, brutal great Babylon of a place, & if one doesn't like it very much, one must hate it: but fortunately I like it." He lauded Paris as the happy "city of vice" (quoted in Kaplan, 219, 253) but thought that Rome in particular made any long-term return to American impossible: "At last—for the first time—I live. I went reeling and moaning thro' the streets, in a fever of enjoyment" (quoted in Lewis, 212). In the summer of 1872, James resolved to remain abroad solely for the capacity Europe offered for his survival. "I feel as if my salvation, intellectually and literarily, depended upon it" (quoted in Lewis, 226-27). In Italy James could dwell on art, interpreting the works of Michelangelo and Da Vinci. Rome "quietly, profoundly, intensely delights and satisfies." (quoted in Lewis, 227).

What one senses above all in James's response to Europe is the appreciation of social freedom by a young man who until going there had known only confinement. In contrast, many Americans found Europe frighteningly unfamiliar. While James did not participate in all the sensuality (and sexuality) offered to him in Europe, and particularly in Italy, he could appreciate the allure. The difference between his response and that of a typical American might correspond to the difference between the person of imagination and the literalist so often devoted to puritanical mores. For the marginal male who imagined a freer existence beyond patriarchal restrictions, Europe offered considerable promise.

According to Adeline Tintner, James sought the cosmopolitan sensibility that exorcised cultural bounds altogether. He idealized the American expatriate as the one person of the Western world who could borrow from all European cultures because he had so little to bear from his own. A European always remains fundamentally French, German, Italian, or some other nationality. Only an American "who has been reared and educated in Europe" can "want or hope to be European without belonging to a specific nationality" (Tintner, *Cosmopolitan World*, 2). Many roots strapped the native European in prejudices—Catholicism, monarchism, and anti-Semitism to name a few. James boasted that Americans can "claim property wherever we find it" (*Letters*, I, 77), and so he turned to Europe to claim things his American forebears had left behind, rather than remain in America where patriarchal decisions circumvented his own.

Indeed, the specter of American provincialism followed him wherever he went. He found Americans abroad more often than not to be "vulgar, vulgar,

vulgar," and he noted "their ignorance—their stingy, grudging, defiant attitude toward everything European—their perpetual reference of all things to some American standard or precedent which exists only in their own unscrupulous wind-bags—and then our unhappy poverty of voice, of speech and of physiognomy—these things glare at us hideously" (quoted in Kaplan 109). This alter ego, the American he might have been, haunted him throughout his life and appears in his fiction in the form of a ghost in the short story "The Jolly Corner."

James's efforts to escape the influence of fathers, both literal and symbolic, would be reflected in his fiction. At the same time, he attended to the significant absences of fathers; his work is replete with absent authority figures who haunt their sons in their absence. As both William and Henry Senior exercised control over Henry Junior in their absence, so James struggled in his fiction with the complex nature of a father's absence.

One critic has commented that "the absent father" plays a "primary" role in James's fiction; absence is the father's "most arresting attribute" (Boren, *Eurydice*, 29). In *The Portrait of a Lady*, for example, Daniel Touchett, while physically present, strikes the reader as emotionally absent. In Daniel, James portrays a character who is more mother than father, having transferred the duties of disciplinarian and guardian to Mrs. Touchett. Ralph's "father, as he had often said to himself, was the more motherly; his mother, on the other hand, was the more paternal, and even, according to the slang of the day, gubernatorial" (*Portrait of a Lady*, 35). Daniel Touchett possesses that stereotypically feminine fragility that confines him to his bed, making him effectively absent. While enormously successful in all the token duties of the male businessman, Daniel has, in intellectual and emotional engagement with his son, relatively little to offer. Of him it is said, "There were certain differences he never perceived, certain habits he never formed, certain mysteries he never understood" (37). Daniel Touchett's business success has been followed in England by a refusal to engage himself socially except in limited ways. While Ralph finds this intentional naiveté endearing, James wryly suggests a negative quality: Daniel "was much of the time unconscious; he slept a great deal; he rarely spoke" (165).

Ralph Touchett's father is one of several absent fathers in James's fiction. *The Princess Casamassima*, a novel about orphans and illegitimacy, depends in several ways on the absence of the father. The marginal male, Hyacinth

Robinson, might have shared in wealth and an honorable reputation had his father not failed to acknowledge him. As it stands, Hyacinth's frantic search for identity stems almost exclusively from paternal neglect as he oscillates between the poles of acknowledged illegitimacy and the wished-for fame and riches of legitimacy.

Hyacinth's father was absent in part because he refused to acknowledge his son. This intentional neglect of his son leads to his literal absence, when Hyacinth's mother murders his father out of revenge for his inattention. His death ends the possibility of communication between father and son, thereby confirming Hyacinth's orphan status: after his mother's imprisonment, Hyacinth has in effect "no family" (*Princess Casamassima*, 202).

Even if he were alive, Hyacinth's father would still be absent from his son because he is obscured in mystery, his life mired in such conflicting reports that it is difficult to distinguish truth from falsehood. For example, Miss Pynsent habitually recounts Lord Purvis' history as a "monstrous farce" (169), persistently exaggerating accounts of Hyacinth's father to make him the worst of demons, the parent of Hyacinth's woes. On other occasions, Miss Pynsent and others simply refuse to say anything at all about Hyacinth's father, and lies are replaced with silence, serving only to intensify the father's absence.

In "The Pupil," James vividly illustrates just how absent a father can be even in times of family crisis. The story explores the degree to which a father can fill every social expectation yet remain essentially uninvolved in his son's affairs. "The Pupil" is about social constructs, a record of a family's ability to maintain a veneer of respectability while suffering the worst forms of debasement.

Morgan qualifies as marginal out of a hypersensitivity to abuses at the hands of his family, coupled with his infatuation with his male tutor and his marked physical frailty. Socially, physically, and sexually unfit for the aggressive world of men, Morgan is doomed from the outset. His condition foreshadows his early death in a home where fatherhood defines itself not by biological or emotional ties but by the facade of social convention. Morgan lacks interaction with his father because, as in so many of James's works, the father figure serves only to fill a space designated by society. Mr. Moreen epitomizes fatherhood in a culture where a father's power is "derived on delegated power," where "only social consensus makes it into a rightful one" (Bleikasten, "Fathers," 118).

The freedom from responsibility that Mr. Moreen enjoys is as the freedom of the gods, never reporting to anyone about his mysterious activities, an irresponsibility that might be categorized as a father's "extravagance" (Rowe, "Screwball," 21). At the beginning of the tale, Mr. Moreen is physically absent, leaving his wife to manage the family. Apologizing for her husband's absence, Mrs. Moreen blithely reveals that he "has been called to London for a week" ("Pupil," 220). This early absence is one of many in the story—just as the father is absent when the tutor arrives, so he is absent at the announcement of Pemberton's leaving and at most negotiations of Pemberton's salary. More significantly, he rarely spends time with Morgan.

Mr. Moreen is also absent in his lack of personal history—neither the reader nor Pemberton knows what he does while he is away from home. All that is known is the family's pitiful financial condition. Some portion of him—information about his past, what he does in London, his future plans, what he thinks of his children or his wife—is always missing, and in this way he is absent even when he is standing in the room. This absence of definition is perhaps best symbolized by the ribbon he wears in his buttonhole, emblematic of past deeds but signifying nothing in particular. What the ribbon does indicate is the air with which Mr. Moreen, a "perfect man of the world," carries himself. As much as any father in James's fiction, Mr. Moreen bears the mark of the conventional father who seems more "a stranger and an intruder" than a natural part of the family (Bleikasten, 117.) This is the great puzzle of "The Pupil," and highlights a major theme of the book: What purpose can a father serve for his son when he does nothing more than maintain appearances?

Mr. Moreen is also absent by an implied physical and spiritual insubstantiality. At home he lingers, silent and shrouded in dim passageways and arcades. On the rare occasions when he presents himself before Pemberton, he mumbles a few words and then, like a ghost, "melted into space," leaving Mrs. Moreen to speak on his behalf. "Mr. Moreen could . . . disappear for several days" (233). He performs for the moment, exhibiting the requisite characteristics of a gentleman. His urbanity is so perfect as to be sinister, suited to any and all occasions—a visit to a museum, a complaint from his son's tutor, his son's death. At Morgan's death, Mr. Moreen is visibly shaken, but quickly returns to his customary urbanity, like the "rich vacant American" Mr. Granger, looming large as an idea but lacking in substance.

In *The Turn of the Screw*, James uses the young nephew, Miles, in a marginalized role similar to that of Morgan Moreen. Miles suffers from a hypersensitivity and precocity that make him susceptible to circumstance and finally destroy him. He is the "little gentleman," emotionally and intellectually mature beyond his years, yet physically a child and in this way a marginal figure. As much as any story by James, *The Turn of the Screw* demonstrates the importance of the absent father to the narrative; the story could not have happened but for the existence of males *in absentia*. If, as Roland Barthes states in *Plaisir de Texte*, "every narrative is a staging of the (absent, hidden, or hypostatized) father" (quoted in Davis, "Barthelme," 181), then *The Turn of the Screw* is an exposé of this cultural and literary phenomenon. In the late 1890s, James explored in *The Turn of the Screw* and in *What Maisie Knew* what it means to be a child of absent parents. In a study of marginal males, Miles offers more appropriate material, but both novellas offer a study of what was a cultural norm then and is perhaps becoming so again today. Parents bear children, and for reasons socially acceptable among the upper classes (perhaps less socially acceptable now), leave their children to the care of a single parent or surrogate. Such an experience can be tragic, but also educational in the case of Maisie, and liberating in the case of Miles.

In *The Turn of the Screw*, absent real fathers—like absent symbolic fathers—intensify Miles's marginalization and ultimate demise. The absence of father figures leads to Miles's "corruption" at the hands of Quint in what more than one James scholar has called a "homoerotic sexual adventure" (Kaplan, 414). As Mrs. Grose tells the governess, "The master went, and Quint was alone" with Miles, and "in charge" of his fate (*Turn of the Screw*, 229). Miles's legacy of absent fathers begins with the death of his real father, a military man. The children then go to stay with their grandparents, who die soon thereafter, leaving the children to their uncle. The uncle "had done all he could; had in particular sent them down to his other house" (199). After the uncle sends Miles and his sister to the country estate, there is good reason to believe that Miles never sees his uncle (his adopted father) again. The uncle makes the rules but is never present to witness the effect of his rules on the children.

The uncle not only absents himself from Miles, but assures that Miles and his sister are absent from him. In the tradition of *in loco parentis* shared by Maisie in *What Maisie Knew*, Miles is to know more detachment than love from his uncle, just as Maisie must acknowledge her natural parents' repugnance for the reality of raising children. Miles's uncle gives the governess one command only, a command which serves not his charges, but himself, that the governess "never trouble him—but never, never: neither appeal nor complain nor write about anything" (201). Even on the occasions when Miles's behavior demands the uncle's involvement, the uncle goes to great lengths to guarantee that he will not be involved. The letter from Miles's schoolmasters goes unopened and is sent directly to the governess with the note, "This, I recognise, is from the headmaster and the headmaster's an awful bore. Read him, please; deal with him; but mind you don't report. Not a word. I'm off!" (207). The only thing the letter assures is the uncle's freedom from responsibility.

The refrain of the uncle's commands is an abdication of his role as father. He absents himself as effectual father, being present in name only, and becoming for the reader and little Miles first a disembodied voice and then a silence, speaking only to ensure his privacy. For Miles he ceases to exist even as a voice—he "never wrote" to his nephew (274).

In fact, as James crafts the story, the uncle's very existence becomes dubious. Is he a figment of the governess's imagination? James here tests the limits of both presence and absence. In this tale, the father figure is absent not only physically, but also in the way he reaches the reader's imagination, for the reader must penetrate the filters of multiple storytellers. The uncle is filtered through the governess, who has reported by letter to the storyteller, who in turn relates the story to the narrator, who finally informs the reader. In turn, the governess may be separated into at least three personas: first, "the one whose experiences at Bly provide the *histoire* or *fabula* of the narrative," second, the "writing governess" whose written recollections some thirty years later provide its *discours*, and third, "the older and wiser but still young governess" whom the reader meets only briefly some ten years after the events at Bly (Poole, *Henry James*, 146). This baffling series of narrative frames makes even present characters seem unreal, let alone the physically absent uncle. A statement the governess makes about Quint might also be said of the uncle: "He was there or was not there: not there if I didn't see him" (*Turn of the Screw*, 224). Like Quint, the uncle assumes the qualities of a phantom, making the reader doubt his existence.

The Ambassadors, like *The Turn of the Screw*, tells the reader more about symbolic fathers than literal fathers; indeed the surprise element in this story about a middle-aged man is that there should be any father at all. Lacanian fathers in this novel are several, assuming the form of whoever speaks on behalf of the patriarchy. From her imperial seat at Woollett, Mrs. Newsome represents patriarchal law and order, signifying what Strether calls "the ideal" (*Ambassadors*, 51), meaning the Puritan ideals of New England; she is the only woman Strether knows who has never lied, for "to lie was beyond her art" (68). Strether uses the little green book, Mrs. Newsome's *Review*, as an example of her New England ideals, even while he admits, "I don't begin to have her faith" (51). In fact Mrs. Newsome's ideals are a major stumbling block for Strether, who has long been imprisoned by her world view. In reference to his servitude to Mrs. Newsome, he confides in Maria Gostrey, "Don't I when I lift the last veil?—tell you the very secret of the prison-house" (51).

Waymarsh functions as another symbolic father, reprimanding Strether just as Mrs. Newsome would if she were in Paris. For Strether, Waymarsh has always represented the extreme of New England rigidity, embodying "the very voice of Milrose," which far exceeds Woollett in maintaining "the real tradition" (31). James never explicitly defines the real tradition, but it is whatever Europe is not: where Europe is antique and immoral, America is patriarchal and Protestant. Strether admires the security of Waymarsh's position in this "real tradition"; he views it as one more sign of Waymarsh's success, though he is at the same time terrified by the inflexibility of his friend's morality, a "rage" and an "opposition" (159) against the lifestyle Strether adopts in Europe. Strether must steel himself against the "shock" of the man (19). What frightens Strether most is that his companion has a missionary purpose: "To save you, poor old man, to save you; to save you in spite of yourself" (224). After weeks of concealing his intent, Waymarsh says to Strether, "I told you so—that you'd lose your immortal soul!" (108).

Sarah Pocock functions as yet another symbolic father in her role as guardian of patriarchal values, standing in for Mrs. Newsome to the point that she becomes Mrs. Newsome's persona. When Strether first confronts Sarah, "it had been for him as if he were dealing directly with Mrs. Newsome" (229). He "could have taken her for Mrs. Newsome while she met his eyes as the train rolled into the station" (208). Her personality in the novel lacks any distinction from Mrs. Newsome's insofar as she and her mother represent the same thing—the Puritan morality of Woollett transmitted by the patriarchy. Sarah is but an oracle of "the real word from Woollett" (216).

Indeed Sarah and Mrs. Newsome speak so forcefully for this received code of behavior that they disempower Woollett males. Strether is mindful of New England men like Jim Pocock who find themselves ostracized from a male-originated system. He says to Madame de Vionnet, "[Jim] understands, you see, that Chad and I have above all wanted to have a good time." Jim, not Sarah or Mrs. Newsome, empathizes with Strether's need for release from a rigid moral code. Jim's "wife and his mother-in-law have, as in honour bound, no patience with such phenomena, late or early" (232). The code voiced by the women of Woollett precipitates in the Woollett male a severe midlife crisis. Strether says, "Men of my age, at Woollett—and especially the least likely ones—have been noted as liable to strange outbreaks, belated uncanny clutches at the unusual, the ideal. It's an effect that a lifetime of Woollett has quite been observed as having."

The patriarchal ideal of the town of Woollett is sufficient to assume its own persona. Strether personifies the town when he says, "Woollett isn't sure it ought to enjoy. If it were it would" (25). The town of Woollett is the Lacanian symbolic father who prohibits Strether from abandoning himself to the pleasures of Paris. Woollett might say, as Waymarsh says to Strether, "Don't do anything you'll be sorry for" (272).

While this patriarchal presence is noteworthy, the *absence* of these powerful presences is perhaps more so, exemplified by the sheer distance of Paris from America. If the Puritan society of New England is the source of patriarchy in the novel, then James carefully absents that patriarchy, or the "father," by never allowing Strether to set foot in America during the narrative. The plot begins with Strether's arrival in London, and ends abruptly as he decides to leave Paris. In addition, the reader gets only pieces of his activities in New England before and after his European experience. Strether reveals only that he has his name printed on the cover of the Woollett *Review,* that his wife and son have died, and that he has been courting Mrs. Newsome. Beyond these facts, his life remains untold, partly to emphasize the enormity of what he has not done as opposed to what he might have accomplished, but also to confine to a distant past and geography the puritanical influences on his life.

Strether himself acknowledges the importance of the geographical distance between Paris and Woollett, imagining the wide gulf of the Atlantic Ocean as symbolic of the emotional and intellectual distance he feels from the source of his ambassadorship. Mrs. Newsome never comes to Europe to see things for herself. "Her tact had to reckon with the Atlantic Ocean, the General Post-Office, and the extravagant curve of the globe" (110). Admittedly there is part of Strether that never wants to see Mrs. Newsome again: "It was only true that if he had seen Mrs. Newsome coming he would instinctively have jumped up to walk away a little" (61).

Unlike Mrs. Newsome, the symbolic father Waymarsh does make it to Paris, but he is still absent in several ways. On numerous occasions, he fails to meet Strether as planned. For example, when Waymarsh neglects to join Maria and Strether after a day of shopping, Waymarsh afterward "told them nothing, left his absence unexplained, and though they were convinced he had made some extraordinary purchase they were never to learn its nature" (41). On another occasion, Waymarsh purposefully passes by Strether at a dinner engagement so he can observe Strether from across the street, allowing him to feel neglected. After a conversation with Chad, Strether again meets with Waymarsh's unexpected absence. "Strether, left alone, looked about, superficially for Waymarsh. But Waymarsh hadn't yet, it appeared, come down, and our friend finally went forth without sight of him" (190). James accentuates the absence of authority figures by concealing the ultimate authority under several ambassadorial layers. Strether is disciplined not by direct contact with Mrs. Newsome, but by Waymarsh and Sarah Pocock, who take orders from Mrs. Newsome, who in turn receives her orders from the patriarchal tradition of Woollett. The seeker of the informing word must turn not to the authorities but to their "ambassadors"—to which the title of the novel refers.

Often patriarchal authority becomes tainted with the personal ambitions of the messengers, making the absence of rightful authorities more strongly felt. With Strether as a child of sorts, and Mrs. Newsome as the paternal stand-in, an embarrassed Strether turns first to Sarah Pocock and then to Waymarsh to ascertain Mrs. Newsome's opinion. He can, however, only doubt the purity of Sarah's or Waymarsh's message and wish for direction from Mrs. Newsome herself. Part of Strether longs for Mrs. Newsome's voice so he can hear the definitive opinion of Woollett concerning Chad and Paris, and his own actions. His final meeting with Sarah makes him realize "the extent of his desire for the real word from Woollett" (216).

Silences render Waymarsh absent, and Strether has come to identify Waymarsh by his "sacred rages" (41), or the "element of stricken silence" (37).

"Waymarsh had always more or less the air of sitting at the door of his tent, and silence, after so many weeks, had come to play its part in their concert. This note indeed, to Strether's sense, had lately taken a fuller tone, and it was his fancy to-night that they had never quite so drawn it out" (183). Waymarsh's silences become so pronounced that he ceases to exist as a companion for Strether, remaining physically in Europe but spiritually returning to America. The silence culminates in his keeping a secret his letter-writing to Mrs. Newsome. On this subject, "nothing had passed between" Strether and Waymarsh (199).

However, patriarchal absence is not to be viewed negatively. James intends this absence as a liberation. In *The Ambassadors*, as in the chronicles of other marginal males, the absence of the "father" to some degree functions as an avenue of freedom for these marginal characters, offering the recipient a momentary reprieve from patriarchal authority.

An earlier example of this freedom from "fathers" appears in *Roderick Hudson*, when Rowland Mallet's hasty retreat to Europe with his male companion Roderick allows their friendship to flourish in a less restrictive society. James makes clear that America would have frowned on such a relationship. For Americans like Mary Garland and Mrs. Hudson, Europe and its artistic tradition pave the road to destruction. Mrs. Hudson sees "no good" in her son's making statues. She pleads with Rowland to watch over her son, with the implication that he should protect Roderick from any tendencies toward decadence. Roderick says of his mother, "She would fain see me all my life tethered to the law, like a browsing goat to a stake" (*Roderick Hudson*, 76). Against this background of puritanical restraint, the marginal male of the story—the misfit Rowland Mallet—leaves for Europe after promising to watch out for Roderick Hudson, though he means something quite different from what Mrs. Hudson intends. As soon as they are on their way, Rowland professes his "open door" philosophy to his younger companion (105), intending as he does to throw open the doors of social and intellectual restrictions and allow Roderick to "live all you can" in the freer atmosphere of old Rome. Rowland hopes to live a life of the immediate and the sensible rather than saving himself for some future reward promised by the status quo. In Europe, he anticipates for himself and his companion a "peculiar refinement of bliss" (52).

With a theme that James develops more fully in *The Ambassadors*, in *Roderick Hudson* he depicts Europe as a playground for the once-confined marginal male. Anticipating a continent free of the peculiarly confining American morality, Rowland tells a doubtful Cecilia that in Europe "I shall be better entertained and shall be therefore, I suppose, in a better humour with life" (52). There Rowland can revel in "the present, the actual, the sensuous—of life in terms of the moment" (159). A much more devoted American, Mary Garland refuses to condone what she sees as European perversity and decadence, evidenced in "pictures, ruins, statues, beggars, monks" (263). On the other hand, Rowland craves European art for emotional and intellectual survival.

Meanwhile, Miles in *The Turn of the Screw* even more overtly celebrates the freedom he has in the absence of fathers. While in the case of Rowland Mallet (and even more so with Lambert Strether in *The Ambassadors*) James shows the middle-aged male enjoying a delayed childhood, in *The Turn of the Screw*, James depicts the mirror image of these marginal males in Miles, an emotional adult in the body of a child. Young Miles symbolizes the spirit of childhood belatedly released in the marginal male at the moment he is freed by patriarchal absence. In an awkward mixture of adult and child, the man-child Miles romps and plays while occasionally (often in the very moment of greatest playfulness) assuming an adult pose of weariness and disillusion, or as the governess puts it, a personage of both "beauty and misery that no words can translate" (*Turn of the Screw*, 292). Called by his governess the "little natural man" (249) and an "extraordinary little gentleman" (292), the man-child Miles by the opening of the story has already discovered the wide berth open to one who appears to have eluded the shadow of the patriarchy. He has successfully eliminated the school "masters" from his life and, with his uncle in London, is left to explore the playground of patriarchal absence.

The governess notices the freedom at Bly: "I learnt something—at first certainly—that had not been one of the teachings of my small smothered life; learnt to be amused, and even amusing, and not to think for the morrow. It was the first time, in a manner, that I had known space and air and freedom, all the music of summer and all the mystery of nature" (214). Were she not to succumb to the role of surrogate lawgiver, she might continue to celebrate the freedom of the place. As it is, she comes to despise the freedom so exploited by little Miles, which she finds frightening and ultimately destructive.

Unlike the governess, Miles craves freedom from the patriarch. Departing radically from the literary tradition of the son wronged by a neglectful father,

James's story of little Miles shows a son (nephew) revelling in freedom from patriarchal strictures. Before the current governess arrived, Miles had enjoyed the decadent Quint. 'The master went, and Quint was alone" (229). Far from assuming responsibility, Quint apparently encouraged licentiousness. Mrs. Grose confirms the governess's worst fears: that Quint let Miles do whatever he wanted. "It was Quint's own fancy. To play with him, I mean—to spoil him. Quint was much too free" (232). Quint and Miles developed "so close an alliance" from being "perpetually together" (246). Beyond the call of the patriarchs—schoolmasters, uncles, fathers—Miles enjoys a wide margin of forbidden pleasures, so horrifying to the governess that she dares not even articulate them. She speaks only in vague terms "of things that man could do. Quint was so clever—he was so deep. . . . There had been matters in his life, strange passages and perils, secret disorders, vices more than suspected, that would have accounted for a good deal more". (233, 234).

Miles plumbs in the world of "depths," "possibilities," and "invention"—the world of uncircumscribed imagination (236, 243). The world without patriarchs endows him with his "grand little air," his "title to independence, the rights of his sex and situation" (276). Despite impending doom, Miles says to the governess, "Oh yes, I've been ever so far; all round about—miles and miles away. I've never been so free" (318).

Still Miles seeks greater freedom. When he says to the governess, "I want to get away," he does not want to get away from Bly so much as he wishes to escape any possible encroachments on his freedom. Far from wanting to return to his old school, he seeks instead a "new field" (290), presumably more free than the "field" he knows.

In "The Pupil," Pemberton and Morgan also benefit from the perennial absence of the father who might have checked their friendship had he been more conscious of his patriarchal duties. While the story seems largely an indictment of inadequate parenting, in fact Mr. Moreen's absence fosters an appealing dependency between tutor and student. Like Miles in *The Turn of the Screw*, the child Morgan carries himself in an adult manner. A reverse image of the adult males who experience a belated childhood, a child like Morgan is the adult trapped in a child's body, too sensitive and "markedly frail" ("Pupil," 253) to endure the pressures of society. Paternal neglect has fostered a "strange superiority" in the boy (247). In Morgan are combined the elements of world-weariness and playfulness, the child as the man, or the man as the child. One reason that Pemberton sees fit to reveal any and all of his "adult" matters to Morgan is that Morgan carries himself as a "little gentleman." In fact he is so beyond his years in intellectual gifts that Pemberton says, "My dear fellow, you're too clever to live" (247). Morgan has rejected his parents' values, instead choosing his own road. As one critic suggests, "The father's absence creates a predicament wherein a son must discover wisdom within the limitations of his own efforts" (Davis, "Critical," 5). Morgan appears to have made independent decisions largely prompted by his father's absence.

Just as Mr. Moreen's neglect created this odd man-child, so the father's neglect promotes the friendship between tutor and student. One reason this relationship occurs is the complete lack of definition concerning Pemberton's assignment. Mr. Moreen leaves Pemberton to his own devices. Is Pemberton to teach, or is he to fill a much larger role in Morgan's life? This is but one example of how Mr. Moreen's negligence is James's key to the story. With no defined tasks, Pemberton is free either to follow in Mr. Moreen's footsteps or to assume a larger role. He decides to exceed expectations. He "would try to be school himself—a bigger seminary than five hundred grazing donkeys, so that, winning no prizes, the boy would remain unconscious and irresponsible and amusing" (227).

Morgan notices how much time Pemberton spends with him: "They leave me with you altogether. You've all the responsibility" (244). This unrestricted time together invites intimacy between tutor and student and, where normally the divisions of power between child and adult would be delineated, in the much larger role Pemberton finds himself in, he must allow Morgan to be privy to adult matters. Where customarily a teacher would never discuss matters of salary with his student, Pemberton discovers that he cannot withhold information from his precocious student. "They were far too intimate" for Pemberton to tell Morgan that certain matters are not for him to hear (236). Their intimacy is such that Morgan begins to value Pemberton as a parent, pleading with Pemberton to run away with him to form an alternate family of sorts. So long as Pemberton is spending so much time with him, "why then should they object to my taking up with you completely?" (244). "I'll go like a shot if you'll take me," Morgan says to him (243). In the absence of the father, Pemberton and Morgan enjoy a freedom that encourages them to fantasize about a world where fathers are extinct.

In a manner similar in some ways to that of the children just mentioned, in *The Ambassadors* Lambert Strether enjoys the freedom of what might be considered a second childhood. Just as Miles and Morgan are in a way disillusioned adults far beyond their years, so Strether in the absence of patriarchal figures becomes the proverbial child in the candy shop, enjoying innocent pleasures that should have been his years before. One instance comes during his friendship with the most jaded of Parisians, Miss Barrace, in whose presence Strether takes up smoking, a pastime he seems never to have experienced before; Miss Barrace supplies him with "a succession of excellent cigarettes." The innocent, even childlike, Strether is just now waking up to the delicious pleasure of an evening smoke. "Strether had never smoked, and he felt as if he flaunted at his friend that this had been only because of a reason. The reason, it now began to appear even to himself, was that he had never had a lady to smoke with" (78). He thinks of smoking as one of Miss Barrace's many enviable "freedoms."

There are other examples of Strether's taking a childish delight in new-found pleasures. Strether delights in the delicious sense of "escape" from the lawgiver Mrs. Newsome; he is "literally running away" from her (33). The morality of Woollett prevents an atmosphere of playfulness, because the Puritan restrictions there make everything serious; however, "turning to Europe, one will find the existence of a truer play-sphere" (Maid, "Playgrounds," 79). When Strether sits in the Luxembourg Garden reading Mrs. Newsome's most recent letter, all the while being distracted by the sights and sounds of Paris, he thinks that "it was the difference, the difference of being just where he was and *as* he was, that formed the escape—this difference was so much greater than he had dreamed it would be" (60). He feels the "escape" again when he goes for a jaunt in the country after Sarah Pocock has left; in the French countryside he is relieved because nobody, particularly Waymarsh, is around to judge him on anything at all—even on his ability to speak French. The "playground" of Europe, a Bakhtinian carnival of sorts, is noticeably free from patriarchal restraints that would burden a New Englander, giving Strether a peace of mind and body he has never known up to that time.

Strether's delayed experience of these adult pleasures typifies the marginal male who has maintained a certain innocence while other adult men are participating in accepted rites of passage. It is as if the marginal male, with his acute sensitivity to the social code established by the patriarchy, resists even relatively innocent pleasures for fear of being punished. Strether's time in Europe becomes then the perfect setting for his delayed childhood, an awakening of consciousness to new sensibilities at age fifty-five "remarkably like that of adolescence" (Yeazell, *Language*, 34). In Europe, Strether enjoys "the immediate and the sensible," as opposed to the patriarchal promise of the adult pleasures of financial and social success (18). He can enjoy a brilliant afternoon with Madame de Vionnet over a "bottle of straw-coloured Chablis" set on "white table-linen" at an "open window" (176).

Strether's stay in Europe also means a new sense of openness; he embraces a "consciousness of personal freedom" (18), choosing to be "independent" and "alone" rather than meeting with Waymarsh (19). He also comes to appreciate the most highly prized of Jamesian treasures—the unconfined imagination. Beyond the shadow of the "fathers," Strether romps in a feast of the imagination. Every turn in the streets of Paris offers Strether food for his fantasies, in marked contrast to the confinement of Woollett where his life was shadowed by Mrs. Newsome. "In Paris the imagination reacted before one could stop it" (69).

Strether's delight epitomizes the joy of the American expatriate male freed from the patriarchal values of Puritanism. While American women in James's fiction often must assume the burden of European gender restrictions, the expatriate American male can enjoy all the benefits of a jaded society while eluding the burden of its history. James seems to have been acutely aware of the unique quality of freedom Europe could offer the male marginalized by America's Puritan leanings.

Despite James's efforts to enhance the freedom of marginal males through the absence of fathers, he still acknowledges the social consequences of such play: the fun must end. Almost without fail, these characters come to a tragic end, as if in punishment for their excesses. Sometimes the payment comes in the form of chronic guilt; or perhaps in precociousness and premature aging when the character shoulders the responsibilities of the absent father; or the punishment may come in the form of death. In the end, the absent father symbolically reappears to discipline the son with some "aggressive paternal gesture" (Davis, "Critical," 15).

In *The Ambassadors*, the punishment for misdeeds committed in the absence of the authorities is something other than death. Indeed the reader could almost wish for Strether's death in place of so much uncertainty. What is certain is the long and painful payment Strether makes with his emotions. He suffers from chronic guilt that appears most intense when the "fathers" are most distant; the more absent the patriarchy is, the more it punishes him.

The absent Mrs. Newsome punishes Strether by haunting his imagination. Indeed, her invasion of his imagination depends on her absence. He sits, "pen in hand with Mrs. Newsome" (102), as if she were at his side. "It was in a manner as if Mrs. Newsome were thereby all the more, instead of the less, in the room, and were conscious, sharply and sorely conscious, of himself, so he felt both held and hushed, summoned to say at least and take his punishment" (247). In corporeal reality she is not a threat, but in her absence she becomes the ghost of Woollett, conjuring up a variety of painful emotions in Strether's mind. His imagination runs wild. "Strether had constantly, in the inmost honour of his thoughts, to consider Mrs. Newsome" (159). Mrs. Newsome's perennial absence withholds her affirmation or approbation; in place of any definition, he endures "imagined horrors" (101).

More specifically, Strether pays for his misdeeds with fear. Despite the absence of authority figures, he anticipates punishment. He hardly knows a moment of calm, because the main source of his punishment is always undefined and in the future. Also, in his first moments in Europe, his joy in his newfound freedom is curbed by a fear of "the shock of Waymarsh" (19). "He winced a little, truly, at the thought that Waymarsh might be already at Chester" (18). The more he experiences the pleasure of absent fathers, the more he fears retaliation. He endures the agony of a "double consciousness," partly of joy and partly of fear (18).

Strether also pays for his freedom with guilt. His "double consciousness" encourages him to enjoy Europe even while he looks back to the moral rectitude of New England. His life becomes a binary path between "shoulds" and "should nots." While he enjoys the company of Maria Gostrey, he feels he "should" be spending time with Waymarsh (24). Maria Gostrey senses his guilt and verbalizes his feelings for him: "You're doing something that you think is not right" (25). Waymarsh's silences implicate Strether without naming his sin, leaving him to wonder what he has done wrong. If only Waymarsh would speak, then Strether might uncover his misdeeds. As it is, in the ambiguity of silence or absence, he pays dearly by suspecting that his actions are "worldly" and "wicked" (39).

The absence of authority invites the imagination to exacerbate the sense of guilt. Before Sarah Pocock arrives, her absence encourages Strether to imagine himself guilty of some vague wrongdoing as he tries to guess the motive for her censure. "She so met his eyes that, his imagination taking, after the first step, all, and more than all, the strides, he already felt her come down on him, already burned, under her reprobation, with the blush of guilt, already consented, by way of penance, to the instant forfeiture of everything" (201). Sarah's absence forces Strether to guess his wrongdoing when he otherwise would have already known his sin. As for Mrs. Newsome, she controls him by never relieving him of guilt. Her power by absence demoralizes him more than any sin he might commit. "He hadn't yet struck himself, since leaving Woollett, so much as a loafer, though there had been times when he believed himself touching bottom. . . . He almost wondered if he didn't *look* demoralised and disreputable" (316).

The absence of authority also translates into a sense of inadequacy. Perhaps he hadn't served faithfully enough as editor of the *Review*, or he has not been aggressive enough in masculine pursuits or community service. A more present authority might recognize and congratulate Strether's accomplishments in Europe, even if these accomplishments vary from anticipated ends. However, absence of authority makes his mission unsatisfying in that he is never validated by the one person who possesses the authority to do so.

Two other tales show marginal males paying with even more than guilt and fear: in the most sinister treatment of the issue of absent fathers, James depicts Morgan Moreen in "The Pupil" and little Miles in *The Turn of the Screw* as paying with their lives. While enjoying the freedom given by a negligent father, Morgan ends up bearing emotional burdens that are quite beyond his capacity. The reader learns early of his fragility; he is "somehow sickly without being 'delicate'" ("Pupil," 219). Morgan is old before his time: "From one moment to the other his small satiric face seemed to change its time of life" (220); he has the attributes of a wise and wizened old man, a "stoic" (227); and he seems intelligent beyond his years, so much so that the family calls him their "genius" (221). His early and painful education, however, is not so much in intellectual issues as in awareness of exploitation, a "kind of homebred sensibility" injurious to his health (227).

Besides paying with poor physical health, Morgan pays with guilt. He sees what his father's neglect has done to the family. Rather than allowing the family to fend for itself, Morgan tries to shoulder the burden of guilt. The father's responsibility is conveniently shifted to the person least able to bear it. Morgan is shamed by his father's shabby treatment of Pemberton, at first escaping self-blame by attributing the family ills to a curse of the fathers of the Moreen line, yet later wondering, "What had their forefathers—all decent folk, so far as he knew—done to them, or what had *he* done to them?" (249). As is typical of the hypersensitive marginal male, guilt haunts the son rather than the father. "To the sons fall all the duties and debts, to the fathers all the prerogatives of power" (Bleikasten, 133). Masked behind Morgan's guilt is a patriarchal system guaranteed to secure the comfort of those in power so long as they respond as "perfect men of the world." By concerted effort, the status quo and the patriarchs who invented it perpetuate each other. Meanwhile, the imperfectly masculine son suffers.

Meanwhile, Pemberton pays for Mr. Moreen's absence and negligence in a very literal way, with money. It is suggested by his quick exit to teach a "wealthier" pupil that Pemberton has not been adequately paid by Mr. Moreen, whose assignment as father of the family is to provide for its material needs. Mr. Moreen either avoids promising to pay the tutor a specific amount, or when he is cornered, "appeals to [Pemberton], on every precedent, as a man of the world" ("Pupil," 238). Mr. Moreen wants Pemberton, as another "man of the world," to understand why he can't expect adequate funds. The father's chronic absence and neglect, as much as it allows Pemberton great freedoms, is also a source of humiliation. Where Pemberton must crawl, scrape, and abase himself just to get enough money to make ends meet, Mr. Moreen is free from unpleasantness. "Pemberton recognized in fact the importance of the character—from the advantage it gave Mr. Moreen. He was not confused or embarrassed, whereas the young man in his service was more so than there was any reason for" (233). Mr. Moreen knows how little he has to risk, having committed the tutor emotionally, saying, as his wife says, "You won't [leave], you *know* you won't—you're too interested. You *are* interested, you know you are, you dear kind man!" (234). The father knows that at bottom it is not money that will keep Pemberton in the Moreen household. Then again, the father might not care one way or the other; he has little to lose since he has invested nothing.

In addition to the punishment of penury, the absence of the father also punishes Pemberton by forcing him to make a large emotional investment in

Morgan. "He utterly committed himself" (223). The Moreens expect Pemberton to invest everything in their son. They are "the amiable American family looking out for something really superior in the way of a resident tutor" (219). As pleasantly intimate as the relationship is between Pemberton and Morgan, the penalty is that Pemberton invests far more emotionally than he can expect in return. Here is the irony of the title "The Pupil," for while Morgan is in formal training under the tutelage of Pemberton, the tutor must learn perhaps the greater lesson about investments and costs in human relationships, about just how well some people play the game. Mr. Moreen is an aficionado, making other people responsible for his own sins and giving vice the appearance of virtue. When he should condemn himself as an abuser of children at the time Morgan becomes ill from parental neglect, he instead congratulates himself on being able to "trust" Mr. Pemberton. "O yes—we can feel that we *can*. We trust Mr. Pemberton fully" (266). When Mr. Moreen is most negligent, he appears most benevolent.

The father never appears more innocent than at his son's death. Pemberton has invited Morgan to live with him, but just when the future looks brightest, Morgan suffers heart failure. Pemberton must stand by helplessly as the physically weak child dies from excitement. Although one may claim that Pemberton is partly responsible for Morgan's death, by prolonging Morgan's suspense about their leaving, ultimately it is Mr. Moreen who finally could have saved Morgan from suffering and death. Instead, the father transfers the sorrow and guilt to Pemberton, whose emotions are invested in a situation where he is powerless. At the end Mr. Moreen can absolve himself of any wrongdoing and take "his bereavement as a man of the world," leaving Pemberton to grieve and repent (267). The father's attainment of absolute freedom without responsibility is the ultimate act of self-empowerment, "the power of extravagance and 'freedom': from labor, from service, from other masters" (Rowe, "Screwball," 18). Pemberton is left powerless, penniless, and grieving for Morgan.

James implies Mr. Moreen's complete culpability. The father's haphazard way of handling family affairs and shifting responsibility to another person appears to be in the blood of the Moreen fathers. Pemberton "was moved to speculate on the mysteries of transmission, the far jumps of heredity" (226). After speculation, the tutor draws the conclusion that "it certainly had burrowed under two or three generations." All the evidence points to the

father and his legacy that throughout the story remain silent and uncommitted, yet possess power to manipulate and punish.

In *The Turn of the Screw*, Miles, like Morgan and Pemberton, must pay the
price of a father's absence. James reminds his reader that a penalty is imposed
on the marginal figure, both for what he has done in the absence of the
authority figure and for what the father has neglected to do. Unlike Morgan
Moreen, Miles has no obvious disability except that he is young in an adult
world. Nonetheless youth is a liability in terms of the father-child dyad
because the patriarch has all the prerogatives. The father's chronological
precedence means for the son "a continual reminder of how little power and
freedom he can negotiate for himself" (Bleikasten, 118).

The uncle, the symbolic father in the story, is perennially absent and
manifests his power by delegation. He promotes his authority through
disguises; "a subtler and more troublesome sort of authority would be that
which *disguises* its power, effectively displacing the signs of its rules to others."
The uncle plays on his incapacity to care for the children, all the while
asserting himself in his "very claim to irresponsibility, even triviality" (Rowe
"Screwball," 3-4). At the moment when he seems most absent, the uncle is
most present, infusing his doctrine through the most devoted of servants, the
governess. She writes, "What I was doing was what he had earnestly hoped
and directly asked of me, and that I *could*, after all, do it proved even a greater
joy than I had expected" (*Turn of the Screw*, 215).

The conflict that arises from the uncle's absence is the conflict of authority,
misconstrued in both Miles's misinterpretation of the freedom he thinks he will
enjoy and in the governess's vision of her "supreme authority" (200). The uncle
promises the governess complete authority—"the vision of serious duties" (200);
she thinks, "I was strangely at the helm" (207). In reality, she has "no real social
power" (Rowe, "Screwball," 6). The uncle deprives her of any recourse to correct
the problems she sees; ultimately she and everyone else must answer to the uncle
because he alone is the patriarch. The uncle's very prohibition against her telling
him anything demands the governess's obedience and submission to his will.
Only after leaving the estate can she finally see the powerlessness of her
situation; she thinks belatedly, "To my present older and more informed eyes it
would show a very reduced importance" (206).

The problems at Bly reach such an extent that even Miles longs for his
uncle's return. While he at first enjoyed the freedom at Bly, the governess's

false authority has become oppressive. Because the uncle's solitary command has been one of absolute silence, the question for both the governess and Miles is how to let the uncle know that he needs to return to Bly. Miles says to the governess, "You'll have to *tell* him—about the way you've let it all drop: you'll have to tell him a tremendous lot" (290). The governess likewise worries about what she will say. The uncle's command of silence creates only tension, punishing everyone at the estate and finally killing Miles. If the uncle had permitted some sort of communication, the boy's death might have been avoided.

In addition to the silence of his charges, the uncle wields authority by his own silence. If only he would speak, the questions that haunt characters and reader alike might be answered. However, his prohibition implies that he will be as silent as his subjects. The governess is left to her own devices to solve the mystery of Bly. Because of her employer's reticence, she is forced in her ignorance of the situation to make hasty accusations, assuming the worst about Miles. She thinks, "There was but one sane inference: some one had taken a liberty rather monstrous" (221). Small wonder then that Miles yearns finally for the uncle's return. The uncle's delegation of responsibility succeeds only in promoting false accusations that punish everyone accept the person who is most responsible—he himself.

The governess is left to invent Miles's crime, engineering psychological torture and ultimately physical punishment. Michel Foucault treats the subject of the modern criminal and the modern prison, surmising that Western culture today punishes its citizens not for the monstrosity of specific crimes but rather on the basis of established reputations of incorrigibility. The most extreme measure, capital punishment, depends less upon "the enormity of the crime itself than [upon] the monstrosity of the criminal" (Foucault, *History of Sexuality*, 1:138). Foucault suggests that authorities often spend considerable energy, therefore, creating a criminal in order to prove a person deserving of a particular punishment. By "making" the criminal, society may actually incite more than discourage criminal behavior. In the scenario established by James in *The Turn of the Screw*, Miles epitomizes the young man made to pay for crimes he might not have committed had he not been labeled a criminal, brainwashed into becoming an accomplice to his own destruction, ready to admit his own guilt to appease the governess. After considerable interrogation, Miles admits, "When I'm bad I *am* bad" (264).

Miles "literally bloomed so from this exploit that he could afford so radiantly to assent" (265). The governess, convinced of Miles's guilt, sanctions the most extreme punishment—death. Before his death, she senses his fear and is pleased, writing, "It was as if he were suddenly afraid of me—which struck me indeed as perhaps the best thing to make him" (319). In the end Miles dies and the governess abandons her position at Bly, while Miles's uncle remains detached and untainted.

In *The Turn of the Screw*, "The Pupil," *Roderick Hudson*, *The Portrait of a Lady*, *The Princess Casamassima*, and *The Ambassadors*, James explores the effect of absent fathers on the marginal male "child," as he does with the female child in *What Maisie Knew*. On the one hand, the marginal male thrives in a rarefied atmosphere of diminished patriarchy where he doesn't suffer persistent blame or castigation. In this respect, the absence of fathers offers another avenue for these males to empower themselves through full expression of their marginality. James's portrayal of such characters such as Morgan, Strether, and Miles shows them relishing this freedom. Strether enjoys a jaunt in the French countryside where he can speak his broken French without fear of ridicule; Miles enjoys the vast spaces of Bly so long as they are free of patriarchal discipline. This sense of almost childish glee at a fatherless freedom applies to James's marginal figures who have felt hampered by social expectations. James's own situation illustrated the urgency of finding a free field of exploration. James found Europe to be his consolation, where he could reside beyond the land of his fathers; for James, Puritan provinciality negated any possibility of psychic survival in America.

However, he cautions his readers about the impossibility of escaping the patriarchy. Absent fathers must not be equated with freedom from discipline, as the marginal male ultimately confronts the reality of disciplinary actions for his "excesses" because he lives in a society whose every social, moral, and political code operates on the assumption that the father must be obeyed. So long as the marginal male resides in a community, he pays a price for his difference. The bizarre deaths of Miles and Morgan Moreen hold great significance when read as symbols of the condition of marginal figures who enjoy freedom for a time, but who consistently pay for their "crimes."

The absence of the father is, then, a somewhat strange and oblique motif in James's fiction. A common feature in many novels and stories, this absence appears to be more than accidental. By implication James shows dissatisfaction with the cultural system, for absent fathers are but placeholders, existing in name only, yet wielding power simply because society has endowed them with it. James reminds his readers how difficult the struggles of marginal figures will be in a culture circumscribed by the father.

Conclusion

James shared with many of his literary successors a belief that sexuality warrants serious treatment in the modern novel if that genre is to remain relevant to the younger generation.[1] While he respected his predecessors for their appropriate reticence on matters of sexuality, he recognized the need to follow a different path as the imaginative chronicler of a new era. James attempted to answer the conflicting calls of decorum and desire, each importunate as the representative voice of his age. On the one hand, decorum beckoned as the last stronghold of virtue in the Victorian Age, while sexuality demanded its due after decades, even centuries, of Puritanical restraint. James's work is witness to the power of each, the one respecting the other, meaning that his characters are emblems of respectability while at moments they can barely contain their desire.

The varied chronologies of James's marginal males can be read as decorous representations of society or as revelations of pent-up desire that threaten to rend the social fabric with their honesty. In *The Ambassadors*, Lambert Strether's journey to Paris could be his first acquaintance with the elegance and refinement of the Old World, or it could signify psychic eruptions that portend the destruction of Strether's Woollett identity. *The Turn of the Screw* could be a ghost story told by a fire on Christmas Eve, or perhaps it is a terrifying world of sexual abnormality where characters search in vain for social moorings. Ralph Touchett could be physically ill, or his illness might be the fortunate pretext for some secret longing. John Marcher's mental journey may be nothing more than nostalgia for love lost, or it could be the rumbling of sexual desires that intend his psychic dissolution.

James's world is composed of doubles that ask to be examined both from without and within. To see James as only the exquisite representative of a bygone golden age is to neglect his complex approach to human psychology. Readers who approach James's work romantically are apt to find characters like Lambert Strether of *The Ambassadors* or John Marcher of "The Beast in the Jungle" unappealing and even tawdry when compared with the typically masculine heroes drawn by other writers. James's work taken in its entirety doesn't invite every reader, in part because of stylistic difficulty, but also because the difficulty fails to offer expected rewards; romantic expectations generally meet with disappointment in James's fiction. In the case of his marginal males, what starts as a likely romance often dwindles into something less glamorous. The quiet halls of Madame de Vionnet's Paris home or Maria Gostrey's cozy quarters are transformed into spaces of erotic potential sans romantic intent; Lambert Strether has had all along his own peculiar aims that circumvent the reader's expectations of conventional romance.

James's encouragement of eccentric behavior suggests a political tendency to proclaim individual autonomy over social tyranny, yet his art seems remarkably complacent, certainly not "revolutionary" in the full sense of the word. This is because politics often promote an ideology that itself depends upon conformity as much as any entrenched social convention, and so undermines individual autonomy. *The Princess Casamassima* and *The Bostonians* represent James's rare attempts to conjoin art with politics in an explicit fashion.[2] Even these novels question the integrity of political ideals that insist on community at the expense of the individual.[3] Outside these exceptions, any revolutionary motive on his part listened more to the voices of individual sufferers than the unified voice of organizers (like the unsympathetically drawn Paul Muniment in *The Princess Casamassima*).

This is not to say that James's work is apolitical. Far from it—his work frequently implodes in a hushed frenzy of private rebellion, exemplified in his marginal males. These characters by their very existence challenge the status quo: they devote the majority of their energy not to public life, but to marginal activities whose source is the imagination. Though their rebellion survives only in secrecy, these characters are politically active as they create zones of difference that defy authority. Moreover, the author's artistic rendering makes their private experiences public. James's narrative favoring of the marginal individual translates into a defiance of tyranny and an advocacy of a world view that accommodates difference.

Some people cannot sympathize with lives and cultures different from their own. The unimaginative person is content to remain within the limited sphere of his or her experience and so cannot understand those of different stations. For James, because morality means to see and to know, a lack of imagination is sinful: "I have an inalienable mistrust of the great ones of the earth," he said, "and a thorough disbelief in any security with people who have no imaginations" (quoted in Edel, 179). People without imagination, including the "great ones" of the earth, impose their way of life on others. To be genuinely kind necessitates an appreciation of the complex life within every person.

James's morality of the imagination approves of the marginal male, whose survival depends on his imaginative powers. Of necessity the marginal male masters conventional appearances, and equally of necessity he creates a private existence. Lambert Strether of *The Ambassadors* exemplifies this double existence of decorum and rebellion. On one hand, he courts the favor of the pinnacle of normalcy, Mrs. Newsome. However, his arrival in Europe frustrates his attempts to live a conventional life, for there he can no longer deny his private desires, which all along have shaped his existence. Strether must struggle with these inner impulses that contradict everything he has learned. Like the myriad voices in Paris that elude "prompt discrimination," Strether's desires are manifold, carrying him in directions that are at times bizarre.

James nurtures marginal behavior in characters such as Strether by providing them with every amenity. One amenity is the marginal male's growing awareness of the potential of language. Strether hears in the many voices of Paris an element that undermines his Woollett mode of existence. He proceeds from a moment of crisis upon his arrival in Europe to a full-fledged awareness of the dual capacity of language to serve or subvert social convention, subsequently replacing the linguistic traps of Mrs. Newsome's oracles with an articulation of his chosen life as bachelor. His last decisions regarding language occur as he informs Maria Gostrey to say nothing to Madame de Vionnet about his having forgiven her. He is now in control of language, no longer willing to help the world with his conversationality.

In addition, Strether's move to Europe frees him just long enough from his American "fathers" to allow him to realize his independent self. At first feeling demoralized by the European experience, he lets his imagination take charge and experiences the delights of a second youth—his first cigarette, lonely explorations through the streets of Paris, and a new awareness of sexual intimacy as manifested in Chad and Madame de Vionnet. However, James cautions the reader that for the marginal male life is never entirely free from patriarchal authority; marginality exists always in relation to the prevailing social norm. In spatial terms, the marginal character enjoys only the spaces unguarded by society. Narrow or spacious, his habitat only seems free as the father deigns not to notice.

The marginal male's most frequent posture is the glance over the shoulder to see if the punishing patriarch is watching, a look backward in time because what he fears is what he has been taught to fear, and backward in space because his thoughts are ultimately dominated by the society he is running from, rather than any personal goal he is running toward. While Strether's greatest pleasure comes from the ecstasy of escape, his agony comes from a realization that his escape is never complete. In fact, the Father's power is perhaps greater in absence because the punishment is threatening, part of an undefined future rather than the known and accepted present. Strether lives in fear of the patriarchy as symbolized by the absent yet present Mrs. Newsome and Waymarsh, and his fear continues as he anticipates the fear of the unknown upon his return to America.

For this reason, James assures his readers that the only lasting comfort for the marginal male lies in the imagination. The man at the margins depends on a self-composed fiction that can withstand the onslaught of a world bent on the destruction of sexual dissidents. The issue for men of alternative masculine behavior is how to compose a fiction that answers to their difference rather than placing their faith in a fiction that falsely promises them a place in the world of standard masculinity. How successfully can Strether, for example, internalize his own model of nonaggression while all around him he sees and admires men whose success depends on exactly such masculine aggression. Strether's world is uniquely other in his self-imaging as a nursemaid, as a young boy or girl, and as an emotional rather than a sexual companion to women. In Strether, James tests the limits of nonaggression in the male, asking to what extent a man can surrender the model of male aggression and still remain in control.

In moving from a dominant to a marginal perspective, James redefines old concepts. For instance, "power" according to the Jamesian model does not mean the domination of others, but rather personal autonomy. The empowered marginal person quietly creates a private world suitable to the self, rather than forcing change in others. As for the concept of masculinity, James's fiction tells a very different story from the one repeated in society. Masculinity for James knows no stereotype, for it is based upon individual interpretation. On the one hand, his approach frees up the concept of masculinity to be applied to anyone of either gender; James favors the "sexual range" referred to in *The Ambassadors*. On the other hand, his standard is actually much more rigorous than the model imposed by society, which mistakenly assumes that outward signs such as physique, dress, and vocal pitch denote masculinity; instead, James's "successful" masculinity relies on the individual's having successfully written a manly text to his own satisfaction. According to James's definition, few marginal males are thoroughly masculine, because they fail to internalize fully their own masculine fictions. For instance, Rowland Mallett of *Roderick Hudson* and Lambert Strether of *The Ambassadors* both admire men who are more acceptable in society's terms of masculinity than they are. Thus, they still believe in an external masculine ideal.[4] James's message seems to be that society's textbook for masculinity is difficult, if not impossible, to forget.

A study of marginality in James's texts also asks the reader to expand what it means to be sexual. In his study of male sexuality in Victorian England, Richard Dellamora stresses the need to accommodate sexual behaviors of the Victorian Age that do not seem to fit sexual categories of today (Dellamora, *Masculine Desire*, 218). For instance, just because a man does not have sex with another man does not mean that he cannot somehow share in the homosexual experience. For James and his marginal characters, this translates into the recognition that sexuality includes more than the act of sex; it is a way of life. Sexual behavior is, in the words of Michel Foucault, "a certain style of existence, . . . or an art of living" (Foucault, "Sexual Choice," 11).

Sexuality is also a way of seeing. The sexual difference known to marginal males alters their world view. To quote from a sexually marginal character in E. M. Forster's *Maurice*, "I don't judge . . . with eyes of the normal man. There seem two roads for arriving at Beauty—one is in common, and all the world has reached Michelangelo by it, but the other is private to me and a few more.

We come to him by both roads." Perhaps the sexually marginal male not only sees differently, but sees more.[5] Because of his double existence, one public and one private, he sees from both common and private perspectives. His survival depends on the watchful gaze. Sexually marginal people find meaningful what the majority finds meaningless, beset as they are "by signs, by the urge to interpret whatever transpires, or fails to transpire . . . , in the momentary glimpse, the scrambled figure, the sporadic gesture, the chance encounter, the reverse image, the sudden slippage, the lowered guard. In a flash meanings may be disclosed, mysteries wrenched out and betrayed" (Beaver, "Homosexual Signs," 104).

The marginal male has perhaps all gone "to eye." He is not a type so much as a vision that can never be fully realized. Because the society he lives in governs the context of the "real," the marginal male at best composes a believable fantasy. In the introduction to the New York edition of *The Ambassadors*, where James talks about the straining motion of his creation Lambert Strether, he might be talking about any number of characters who strain after something that at best can exist only in their dreams. "Art and sex are analogous activities since both are projections of fantasy" (Beaver, 106). James's marginal males epitomize the beauty of projection because their private fantasies are really not private at all, but mirror the wishes of a society too long repressed.

NOTES

Introduction

1. I refer here to a recent trend toward reinvestigation of James's morality, not entirely unlike that which occurred at the first appearance of the author's work. Donna Przybilowicz and Alfred Habegger exemplify this recent reexamination-turned-reevaluation of James's commitment (or lack thereof) to sexual and gender norms.

2. I am by no means the first to claim James as a modernist. See R. W. Short's "The Sentence Structure of Henry James," in *American Literature* 18 (1946), 71-88. He argues that "James was very little of a realist." See also John Carlos Rowe's *The Theoretical Dimensions of Henry James,* concerning "the high-modernist Henry James, whose destiny always seemed to end in the intricacies of his late style" (Rowe, *Theoretical Dimensions,* 11). Jonathan Freedman links James to modernism and even more so to postmodernism: "Henry James transform[ed] the volatile and unstable example of aestheticism in England into that more austere form of aestheticism we call modernism" (Freedman, *Professions,* xvii).

3. To emphasize differences in styles between early and late, I have avoided the New York editions for works written before 1895, as the later revisions of early works are inevitably colored to some extent by James's "dramatic" mode.

Chapter One

1. Chad has by this point convinced Strether to deny, if not abandon, his Puritanism in favor of a more hedonistic lifestyle. As Strether says to Madame de Vionnet, "Chad and I have above all wanted to have a good time" (*Ambassadors,* 232).

2. William's marriage underscored Henry's marginality by prompting a change in his fiction toward a more "feminine identification," which may have reflected a feminization of his personal life (Feinstein, "Singular Life," 322).

3. See chapter 5, "Absent Fathers."

4. Edel's abridged biography of James, *Henry James: A Life,* makes some attempt to explore incidents that he thought best to leave out of the earlier edition while involved parties were still alive. Edel gives his reasoning in the introduction to the abridgment. (References to the abridged biography in this text will be distinguished from the earlier multivolume biography by the absence of volume numbers in the documentation.) See also Fred Kaplan's discussion of Henry's "uneasy passion" for William in *Henry James: The Imagination of Genius, A Biography,* pp. 90-92, 414, 452, 517.

5. This "window straining" episode resembles the famous last scene from Edith Wharton's *Age of Innocence,* when Newland Archer gazes up at Ellen Olenska's apartment window from a park bench below until a servant appears on the balcony and closes the shutter.

6. In his *Ecrits,* Jacques Lacan points to a stage in a person's attempt to achieve the desired object. Lacan locates a suspension in the analysand's memory where activity shuts down. This point in memory—it can go no further in its recovery of the lost object—becomes, by the analysand's obsession on this point, a fetish. "The memory-screen is immobilized and the fascinating image of the fetish is petrified" (Rowe, *Theoretical Dimensions,* 104).

7. Further discussion of Henry's passivity appears in chapter 2, "Private Fictions."

8. *Notes of a Son and Brother* provides abundant evidence of Henry's cognizance of his elder brother's superiority.

9. Further discussion of William as a dominant "father figure" for Henry appears in chapter 5, "Absent Fathers."

Chapter Two

1. Howard Feinstein attributes the vastation to a prolonged anxiety from fourteen years of litigation against Henry Senior's father, William of Albany, over the family estate. Feinstein goes on to say that Henry Senior's sons William and Henry Junior would both be preoccupied with the likelihood of inherited madness, internally predisposed rather than externally derived (Feinstein, "Singular Life," 302).

2. For example, one could describe the dominant culture of the Western world as a monotheistic, paternal community (the "paternal Word") that has enforced its own symbolic system to the destruction of countless smaller voices (Kristeva, *Kristeva Reader,* 140-41).

3. The image of orphan might be professionalized and matured into the image of the aesthete, a person devoted to art and beauty and to an extent orphaned from society—a self-image that James simultaneously resisted and cherished (Freedman, *Professions*, xiv).

4. Medicine on occasion only verified his hypochondria, as when London heart specialist Sir James Mackenzie compared James's imagined heart condition to the imagined horrors of *The Turn of the Screw*: "It is the same with you, it is the mystery that is making you ill. You think you have got angina pectoris and you are very frightened lest you should die suddenly" (quoted in Kaplan, 516).

5. Here I'm referring to "in-between" as defined in this study's introduction.

6. Sister M. Corona Sharp notes a childish aspect in James's interaction with the confidante: "James's numerous maternal friends form a long line of usable mothers for his childish egotism" (Sharp, *Confidante*, xiii). While she condemns James for such childishness, it could be argued that James's ego needed such reinforcement for its very survival. Such confidantes did not merely serve the "child" in James, but assisted him in an elaborate psychological web that protected his marginal self from dissolution.

7. See chapter 3, "Sexual Surprise."

8. Although the contention may be raised that this is the imagination of the narrator and not the character, the unique effort by James to illuminate a single consciousness—that of Lambert Strether in this novel—suggest that Strether is himself conscious of the image of schoolboy, old man, and so on.

Chapter Three

1. Michel Foucault locates the Victorian sexual norm in "the parents' bedroom." Abnormal sexuality, on the other hand, included any behavior "not ordered in terms of generation." Such abnormal or "sterile" behavior, if it insisted on visibility, would be "designated accordingly and would have to pay the penalty" (Foucault, *History of Sexuality*, 3:4).

2. Foucault is quick to add that such "multiplication" of sexual behaviors is possibly a false construct: "It is possible that the West has not been capable of inventing any new pleasures, and it has doubtless not discovered any original vices." What is unique to the nineteenth century, however, is academic discourse about such behavior, which "defined new rules for the game of powers and pleasures. The frozen countenance of perversions is a fixture of this game." (*History of Sexuality*, 1:48).

According to Foucault, sexual perversion would become in the Victorian Age a phenomenon to be studied and manipulated by "those in power."

3. Under the pen of Westphal, homosexuality assumed the form of a clinically diagnosable form of sexuality, transposed from earlier notions of sodomy into "a kind of interior androgyny, a hermaphroditism of the soul." Where "the sodomite had been a temporary aberration" in earlier times, Westphal and his peers established homosexuality as a "species" (Foucault, *History of Sexuality*, 1:43).

4. Whitman denied his bisexuality, though his poetry arguably suggests otherwise.

5. James's disdain for Wilde might also have stemmed from his need to weaken the seemingly irrefutable ground of Wilde's artistic authority, to "proclaim Henry James's own greater knowledge of that ground" (Freedman, *Professions*, 180).

6. The possible exception is *The Finer Grain* (1910), where "sexual seduction and adultery became acceptable constituents" of James's fictional world (Tintner, *Cosmopolitan World*, 279).

7. The four sexual "frauds" of the Victorian Age are: hysteria, onanism, fetishism, and coitus interruptus.

8. This is provocative as it relates to theoretical considerations of authorship. Jacques Derrida claims that a literary work has a life of its own, speaking for itself. Mikhail Bakhtin argues that prose writers own their work stylistically, but that the language used is borrowed from a variety of communities, each insisting on dialogic participation. This insistence of language's autonomy from its author assumes sinister dimensions; the work is "out of control."

9. The homoeroticism of this passage is remarkably similar to that of a passage in a lesser known story, "A Light Man," which Howard Feinstein makes reference to in his study of the sibling rivalry/intimacy of Henry James and his brother William. The passage following describes the blend of competition and affection between two male characters Maximus and Theodore: "The remainder of this extraordinary scene I have no power to describe: . . . how I, prompted by the irresistible spirit of my desire to leap astride of his weakness, and ride it hard into the goal of my dreams, cunningly contrived to keep his spirit at the fever point, so that strength, and reason, and resistance should burn themselves out. I shall probably never again have such a sensation as enjoyed to-night—actually feel a heated human heart throbbing, and turning, and struggling in my grasp; know its pants, its spasms, its convulsions, and its final senseless quiescence" ("Light Man," 367).

Chapter Four

1. James "transgresses" normative language in the manner defined by Julia Kristeva, who contends that common parlance depends on clarity, while poetic language subverts that motive.
2. The diction I use in this sentence illustrates the power of language not only to inform, but to evoke. James's texts demonstrate his sensitivity to the evocative power of language, where the language itself can, for example, suggest sexuality. This evocative quality is appropriate in sustaining the ongoing tension between the marginal male's asexual reality and his sexual fantasies.
3. Again the sexual: James teases the reader in an erotic foreplay of refusal to give the anticipated response.
4. Pemberton is the prototype of the Jamesian marginal male, a bachelor without promise of wife or children who shows a singular affection for his young charge Morgan Moreen. Meanwhile, Morgan Moreen's marginality is derived from his delicate health and his devotion to his teacher, which borders on infatuation. Both Pemberton and Morgan stand outside the power structure created by Mr. and Mrs. Moreen.
5. Lacan's framing of the discussion of language in terms of the real, the symbolic, and the imaginary brings to the realm of psychology what has for twentieth-century linguists since Ferdinand Saussure been a seminal issue, that is, the failure of the signifier (the word) to coincide completely with the signified (the object being described). The speaker's awareness of linguistic failure is necessary for a full manipulation of the language (and, Lacan would say, for a full life).
6. Julia Kristeva associates poetic discourse with immorality as it offends the assumed logic of the dominant morality of Western culture in a linguistic struggle "against Christianity and its representation; this means an exploration of language (of sexuality and death), a consecration of ambivalence and 'vice'" (Kristeva, *Reader*, 50).
7. The ominous threat of too much silence is demonstrated in the case of Hyacinth Robinson, who lacked sufficient verbal definition to create an identity for himself and eventually commits suicide.

Chapter Five

1. By "boundless authority" I mean in the sense of the ancient law of *patria potestas*. Ancient Rome exemplified a society which gave unlimited power to the father to "decide life and death" for his children and his slaves, a

necessary characteristic of sovereign power (Foucault, *History of Sexuality*, 1:135).

2.   Part of this dissatisfaction may be attributed to a widespread phenomenon of the upper classes at that time, where parents raised their children *in absentia*, entrusting them to the care of tutors and governesses. James makes explicit reference to the practice of employing individuals *in loco parentis* in his preface to the New York edition of *What Maisie Knew*.

3.   Not so for the American female, who still paid the high price of womanhood wherever she went.

Conclusion

1.   From "The Future of the Novel." James's relationship with modernism is a complex one, justly treated in Jonathan Freedman's *Professions of Taste*. The favoring of literary discussion of sexuality must not be equated with any unified moral vision, for where both the Modernists and James advocated the introduction of sexual themes, James did not ascribe to the "strenuous moralism" and "questionable metaphysics" that later typified the high modernists such as Eliot who would insist on James as their predecessor (Freedman, *Professions*, 129).

2.   James held particular interest in what he called "the woman question," acknowledging in his essay "The Future of the Novel" that women would indeed play their role in a world many men persist in viewing as exclusively male. His attempt to treat this issue appears in *The Bostonians*. Meanwhile, in *The Princess Casamassima* James gets his hands dirty with the smudge and seaminess of the underworld of nineteenth-century London.

3.   In *The Princess Casamassima*, James involves Hyacinth Robinson in a political revolution, precipitating Robinson's loss of identity and eventual suicide.

4.   Here one enters the unresolved arena of homosexuality, where same-sex fantasies, according to some psychological models, center on the fascination of the insecure male for the imagined masculine superiority of the beloved.

5.   This clairvoyance is not, however, inherent in the condition of marginality, but depends on the awareness that one is marginal in the first place. James's fiction is filled with examples of marginal characters who insist on their normalcy. They see clearly only in moments when they are aware, painfully so, of the limits to their acceptance in the larger community.

BIBLIOGRAPHY

Abbott, Reginald. "The Incredible Floating Man: Henry James's Lambert Strether." *Henry James Review* 11.3 (1990): 176-88.

Ancona, Francesco Aristide. *Writing the Absence of the Father.* Lanham, Md.: University Press of America, 1986.

Anderson, Quentin. *The Imperial Self.* New York: Knopf, 1971.

Anderson, Walter E. "The Visiting Mind: Henry James's Poetics of Seeing." *Psychoanalytic Review* 69.4 (1982/83): 513-32.

——. "The Rape of the Eye." *Psychoanalytic Review* 70.1 (1983): 101-19.

Auchard, John. *Silence in Henry James: The Heritage of Symbolism and Decadence.* University Park: Pennsylvania State University Press, 1986.

Auerbach, Jonathan. *The Romance of Failure: First-Person Fictions of Poe, Hawthorne, and James.* New York: Oxford University Press, 1989.

Bakhtin, Mikhail. *The Dialogic Imagination: Four Essays.* Austin: University of Texas Press, 1981.

Barthes, Roland. *Camera Lucida: Reflections on Photography.* Trans. Richard Howard. New York: Hill & Wang, 1981.

Beaver, Harold. "Homosexual Signs (In Memory of Roland Barthes)." *Critical Inquiry* 8 (Autumn 1981): 99-119.

Bersani, Leo. *The Freudian Body: Psychoanalysis and Art.* New York: Columbia University Press, 1986.

Bleikasten, Andre. "Fathers in Faulkner." *The Fictional Father: Lacanian Readings of the Text.* Ed. Robert Con Davis. Amherst: University of Massachusetts Press, 1981.

Bootzin, Richard R. and Joan Ross Acocella. *Abnormal Psychology: Current Perspectives.* 5th ed. New York: Random House, 1988.

Boren, Linda S. *Eurydice Reclaimed.* Ann Arbor: UMI Research Press, 1989.

Carnes, Mark C., and Clyde Griffin, eds. *Meanings for Manhood: Constructions of Masculinity in Victorian America*. Chicago: University of Chicago Press, 1990.

Clark, Katerina. *Mikhail Bakhtin*. Cambridge, Mass.: Belknap, 1984.

Cohen, Ed. "Foucauldian Necrologies: 'Gay' 'Poetics'? Politically Gay?" *Textual Practice* 2.1 (1988): 87-101.

Cross, Mary. *Henry James: The Contingencies of Style*. New York: St. Martin's Press, 1993.

———. "'To Find the Names': *The Ambassadors*." *Papers on Language and Literature: A Journal for Scholars and Critics of Language and Literature* 19.4 (1983): 402-18.

Crown, Cynthia L., and Stanley Fieldstein. "Psychological Correlates of Silence and Sound in Conversational Interaction." *Perspectives on Silence*. Ed. Deborah Tannen and Muriel Saville-Troike. Norwood, N.J.: Ablex, 1985.

Dauenhauer, Bernard P. *Silence: The Phenomenon and Its Ontological Significance*. Bloomington: Indiana University Press, 1980.

Davis, Lloyd. *Sexuality and Textuality in Henry James: Reading Through the Virginal*. New York: Peter Lang, 1988.

Davis, Robert Con. "Critical Introduction: The Discourse of the Father." *The Fictional Father: Lacanian Readings of the Text*. Ed. Robert Con Davis. Amherst: University of Massachusetts Press, 1981.

———. "Post-Modern Paternity: Donald Barthelme's *The Dead Father*." *The Fictional Father: Lacanian Readings of the Text*. Ed. Robert Con Davis. Amherst: University of Massachusetts Press, 1981.

Dellamora, Richard. *Masculine Desire: The Sexual Politics of Victorian Aestheticism*. Chapel Hill: University of North Carolina Press, 1990.

DuPlessis, Rachel Blau. *Writing Beyond the Ending: Narrative Strategies of Twentieth-Century Writers*. Bloomington: Indiana University Press, 1985.

Eagleton, Terry. *Literary Theory: An Introduction*. Minneapolis: University of Minnesota Press, 1983.

Eakin, Paul John. "Henry James's Obscure Hurt." *New Literary History* 19.3. (1988): 675-92.

Edel, Leon. *Henry James*. 5 vols. Philadelphia: Lippincott; 1953-72.

———. *Henry James: A Life*. New York: Harper & Row, 1985.

Feinstein, Howard M. "A Singular Life: Twinship in the Psychology of William and Henry James." *Blood Brothers: Siblings as Writers.* Ed. Norman Kiell. New York: International Universities, 1983.

Foucault, Michel. *Discipline and Punish: The Birth of the Prison.* New York: Pantheon, 1977.

———. *The History of Sexuality.* 3 vols. Trans. Robert Hurley. New York: Pantheon, 1978-85.

———. "Sexual Choice, Sexual Act: An Interview with Michel Foucault." *Salmagundi* 58-59 (Fall 1982-Winter 1983): 11-24.

Freedman, Jonathan. *Professions of Taste: Henry James, British Aestheticism, and Commodity Culture.* Stanford: Stanford University Press, 1990.

Freud, Sigmund. *The Freud Reader.* Ed. Peter Gay. New York: Norton, 1989.

Gallop, Jane. *The Daughter's Seduction: Feminism and Psychoanalysis.* Ithaca: Cornell University Press, 1982.

———. *Reading Lacan.* Ithaca: Cornell University Press, 1985.

Gay, Peter. *The Bourgeois Experience: Victoria to Freud.* 2 vols. New York: Oxford University Press, 1986.

Goldfarb, Clare R. "Matriarchy in the Late Novels of Henry James." *Research Studies* 49.4 (1981): 231-41.

Gosse, Edmund. *Aspects and Impressions.* New York: Scribner's, 1922.

Gosselin, Chris, and Glenn Wilson. "Fetishism, Sadomasochism and Related Behaviors." *The Psychology of Sexual Diversity.* Ed. Kevin Howells. London: Basil Blackwell, 1984.

Habegger, Alfred. *Gender, Fantasy, and Realism in American Literature.* New York: Columbia University Press, 1982.

———. *Henry James and the "Woman Business."* Cambridge: Cambridge University Press, 1989

———. "The Lessons of the Father: Henry James Sr. on Sexual Difference." *Henry James Review* 8.1 (1986): 1-36.

Hall, Richard. "Henry James: Interpreting an Obsessive Memory." *Essays on Gay Literature.* Ed. Stuart Kellogg. New York: Harrington Park Press, 1985.

―――. "An Obscure Hurt: The Sexuality of Henry James." *New Republic* 28 Apr. 1979: 25-31; 5 May 1979: 25-29.

Hardy, Donald E. "Conversational Interaction and 'Innocence' in James's *The Ambassadors*." *Southwest Journal of Linguistics* 6.1 (1983): 16-22.

Hassan, Ihab. *The Literature of Silence: Henry Miller and Samuel Beckett*. New York: Knopf, 1967.

Irwin, John T. "The Dead Father in Faulkner." *The Fictional Father: Lacanian Readings of the Text*. Ed. Robert Con Davis. Amherst: University of Massachusetts Press, 1981. 147-168.

James, Henry. *The Ambassadors*. New York: Norton, 1964.

―――. *The American*. New York: NAL/Penguin, 1986.

―――. "The Art of Fiction." *The Art of Fiction and Other Essays*. New York: Oxford, 1948.

―――. *The Aspern Papers*. In *The Turn of the Screw and Other Short Novels*. New York: NAL, 1980.

―――. "The Beast in the Jungle." In *The Portable Henry James*. Ed. Morton D. Zabel. New York: Viking, 1979.

―――. "The Figure in the Carpet." *The Figure in the Carpet and Other Stories*. New York: Penguin, 1986.

―――. "The Future of the Novel." In William Veeder and Susan M. Griffin, *The Art of Criticism: Henry James on the Theory and Practice of Fiction*. Chicago: University of Chicago Press, 1986.

―――. "Ivan Turgenev." In William Veeder and Susan M. Griffin, *The Art of Criticism: Henry James on the Theory and Practice of Fiction*. Chicago: University of Chicago Press, 1986.

―――. "The Lesson of Balzac." *The Question of Our Speech* and *The Lesson of Balzac: Two Lectures*. Boston: Houghton Mifflin, 1905.

―――. *Letters*. 4 vols. Ed. Leon Edel. Cambridge, Mass.: Belknap, 1984.

―――. "A Light Man." In *The Tales of Henry James (1864-1969)*. Ed. Maqbool Aziz. Oxford: Clarendon, 1973.

―――. *Notes of a Son and a Brother*. New York: Scribner's, 1914.

————. *The Portrait of a Lady.* New York: NAL/Penguin, 1979.

————. *The Princess Casamassima.* New York: Kelley Press, 1978.

————. "The Pupil." *The Short Stories of Henry James.* Ed. Clifton Fadimon. New York: Random House, 1945.

————. *Roderick Hudson.* New York: Kelley Press, 1978.

————. "Sainte-Beuve." In William Veeder and Susan M. Griffin, *The Art of Criticism: Henry James on the Theory and Practice of Fiction.* Chicago: University of Chicago Press, 1986.

————. "The Tree of Knowledge." In *The Author of Beltraffio and Other Tales.* New York: Scribner's, 1909.

————. *The Turn of the Screw.* In *The Portable Henry James.* Ed. Morton D. Zabel. New York: Viking, 1979.

————. *What Maisie Knew.* Garden City: Doubleday, n.d.

————. *The Wings of the Dove.* New York: Norton, 1978.

Kaplan, Fred. *Henry James: The Imagination of Genius, A Biography.* New York: William Morrow, 1992.

Kaston, Carren. *Imagination and Desire in the Novels of Henry James.* New Brunswick: Rutgers University Press, 1984.

Kristeva, Julia. *Desire in Language: A Semiotic Approach to Literature and Art.* New York: Columbia University Press, 1980.

————. *The Kristeva Reader.* Ed. Toril Moi. New York: Columbia University Press, 1986.

Lacan, Jacques. *Ecrits: A Selection.* Trans. Alan Sheridan. New York: Norton, 1977.

Langevin, Ron. *Sexual Strands.* Hillsdale, N.J.: Lawrence Erlbaum, 1983.

Leeming, David Adams. "An Interview with James Baldwin on Henry James." *Henry James Review* 8.1 (1986): 47-56.

Lewis, R.W.B. *The Jameses: A Family Narrative.* New York: Farrar, Straus, and Giroux, 1991.

Macheray, Pierre. *A Theory of Literary Production.* Trans. Geoffrey Wall. London: Routledge & Kenan Paul, 1978.

Maid, Barry M. *"The Ambassadors*: Henry James's Playground in Paris." *Arizona Quarterly.* 40.1 (1984): 75-84.

Malmgren, Carl. "Henry James's Major Phase: Making Room for the Reader." *Henry James Review* 3.1 (1981): 17-23.

Martin, Robert K. "Knights-Errant and Gothic Seducers: The Representation of Male Friendship in Mid-Nineteenth-Century America." *Hidden from History.* Ed. Martin Bauml Duberman, et al. New York: NAL, 1989.

McWhirter, David. *Desire and Love in Henry James: A Study of the Late Novels.* New York: Cambridge University Press, 1989.

Moon, Michael. "Sexuality and Visual Terrorism in *The Wings of the Dove.*" *Criticism: A Quarterly for Literature and the Arts* 28.4 (1986): 427-43.

Myers, Gerald E. *William James: His Life and Thought.* New Haven: Yale University Press, 1986.

Nelson, Jane A. "The Familial Isotopy in 'The Fox.'" *The Challenge of D. H. Lawrence.* Ed. Michael Squires and Keith Cushman. Madison: University of Wisconsin Press, 1990.

Person, Leland S., Jr. "Eroticism and Creativity in *The Aspern Papers.*" *Literature and Psychology* 32.2 (1986): 20-31.

———. "Henry James, George Sand, and the Suspense of Masculinity." *PMLA* 106.3 (1991): 515-28.

———. "Strether's 'Penal Form': The Pleasure of Imaginative Surrender." *Papers on Language and Literature: A Journal of Scholars and Critics of Language and Literature.* 23.1 (1987): 27-40.

Poole, Adrian. *Henry James.* New York: St. Martin's Press, 1991.

Powers, Lyall H. *Henry James and Edith Wharton: Letters, 1900-1915.* New York: Scribner's, 1990.

Przybylowicz, Donna. *Desire and Repression: The Dialectic of the Self and the Other in the Late Works of Henry James.* New York: Harper & Row, 1985.

Rowe, John Carlos. "Screwball: The Use and Abuse of Uncertainty in Henry James's *The Turn of the Screw.*" *Delta* 15 (Nov. 1982): 1-31.

———. *The Theoretical Dimensions of Henry James.* Madison: University. of Wisconsin, 1984.

Scott, Derrick. "Masculine Ease." *DAI* 48 (1988): 2061A. University of Pennsylvania.

Sedgwick, Eve Kosofsky. "The Beast in the Closet: James and the Writing of Homosexual Panic." *Sex, Politics, and Science in the Nineteenth-Century Novel.* Ed. Ruth Bernard Yeazell. Baltimore: Johns Hopkins, 1986.

Seymour, Miranda. *A Ring of Conspirators: Henry James and His Literary Circle, 1985-1915.* Boston: Houghton Mifflin, 1989.

Sharp, Sister M. Corona. *The Confidante in Henry James: Evolution and Moral Value of a Fictive Character.* South Bend: University of Notre Dame Press, 1963.

Short, R. W. "The Sentence Structure of Henry James." *American Literature* 18 (1946): 71-88.

Showalter, Elaine. *A Literature of Their Own.* Princeton: Princeton University Press, 1976.

Springer, Mary Doyle. "Closure in James: A Formalist Feminist View." *A Companion to Henry James Studies.* Ed. Daniel Mark Fogel. Westport, Conn.: Greenwood Press, 1993. 265-283.

Steiner, George. *George Steiner: A Reader.* New York: Oxford University Press, 1984.

Tannen, Deborah. "Silence: Anything But." *Perspectives on Silence.* Ed. Deborah Tannen and Muriel Saville-Troike. Norwood, N.J.: Ablex, 1985.

Theweleit, Klaus. *Male Fantasies.* Minneapolis: University of Minnesota Press, 1987.

Tintner, Adeline. *The Cosmopolitan World of Henry James.* Baton Rouge: Louisiana State University Press, 1991.

Van Leer, David. "The Beast of the Closet: Homosociality and the Pathology of Manhood." *Critical Inquiry* 15.3 (1989): 587-605.

Veeder, William, and Susan M. Griffin. *The Art of Criticism: Henry James on the Theory and the Practice of Fiction.* Chicago: University of Chicago Press, 1986.

Vieilledent, Catherine. "Literary Pornographics: Henry James's Politics of Suppression." *Henry James Review* 10.3 (1989): 185-96.

Weatherby, W. J. *James Baldwin: Artist on Fire.* New York: Donald I. Fine, 1989.

Weeks, Jeffrey. "Inverts, Perverts, and Mary-Annes: Male Prostitution and the Regulation of Homosexuality in England in the Nineteenth and Early Twentieth

Centuries." *Hidden From History.* Ed. Martin Bauml Duberman, et al. New York: NAL, 1989.

Weinstein, Philip M. *Henry James and the Requirements of the Imagination.* Cambridge: Harvard University Press, 1971.

West, Rebecca. *Henry James.* New York: Henry Holt, 1917.

Wolk, Merla Samuels. *The Safe Space: The Artist Figure in the Novels of Henry James, 1886-1897. DAI* 42 (1982): 4836A. Wayne State University.

Yeazell, Ruth Bernard. "Henry James." *Columbia Literary History of the United States.* Ed. Emory Elliott. New York: Columbia University Press, 1988.

———. *Language and Knowledge in the Late Novels of Henry James.* Chicago: University of Chicago Press, 1976.

———. "Podsnappery, Sexuality, and the English Novel." *Critical Inquiry* 9.2 (1982): 339-57.

Yingling, Thomas E. *Hart Crane and the Homosexual Text.* Chicago: University of Chicago Press, 1990.

Zabel, Morton D. "Introduction." *The Portable Henry James.* Ed. Morton D. Zabel. New York: Viking, 1979.

INDEX

Turgenev, Ivan, 5
tyranny, 58, 103, 108, 128, 156, 157

urbanity, 17, 99, 134

vagueness, 46, 105, 110, 115, 117
Van Leer, David, 7, 61, 63
Veeder, William, 3, 5, 128
Venice, 70
Victorian Age, 6, 72, 80-1, 155, 159,
    163n, 164n
violence, 47, 48-9
voyeurism, 88-91
vulgarity, 131-2

Wagner, Richard, 71
Walpole, Hugh, 22, 40, 73
Walsh, Catherine "Kate" (aunt), 36
Ward, Mary Augusta, 71
Washington Square, 40
Weatherby, W. J., 51
Weeks, Jeffrey, 64, 66, 67
Weinstein, Philip, 41
Wells, H. G., 24, 31
West, Rebecca, 108-9
Westphal, Carl 66, 164n
Wharton, Edith, 24, 25, 27-9, 38, 69,
    70, 162n
What Maisie Knew, 40, 76, 135, 152,
    166n
Whitman, Walt, 67, 164n
Wilde, Oscar, 25, 26, 34, 68, 71, 80,
    102, 164n
The Wings of the Dove, 25, 74, 76
women, 8, 10, 19, 39-40, 45, 49, 53-
    62, 69-70, 74-6, 83-5, 137-40,
    166n

Woolson, Constance Fenimore, 39,
    69, 70

Yeazell, Ruth Bernard, 4, 103, 111,
    118

Zabel, Morton, 103